MEDIA AND COMMUNICATIONS - TECHNOLOGIES, POLICIES AND CHALLENGES

BROADCASTING, THE FCC, INDECENCY AND THE FIRST AMENDMENT:

SCRUTINY AND DEBATE

MEDIA AND COMMUNICATIONS - TECHNOLOGIES, POLICIES AND CHALLENGES

Additional books in this series can be found on Nova's website under the Series tab.

Additional E-books in this series can be found on Nova's website under the E-books tab.

MEDIA AND COMMUNICATIONS - TECHNOLOGIES, POLICIES AND CHALLENGES

BROADCASTING, THE FCC, INDECENCY AND THE FIRST AMENDMENT:

SCRUTINY AND DEBATE

Jacob Jefferson
and
Jennifer S. McGovern
EDITORS

Nova Science Publishers, Inc.
New York

For permission to use material from this book please contact us:
Telephone 631-231-7269; Fax 631-231-8175
Web Site: http://www.novapublishers.com

NOTICE TO THE READER

Additional color graphics may be available in the e-book version of this book.

Library of Congress Cataloging-in-Publication Data
Broadcasting, the FCC, indeceny and the first amendment : scrutiny and debate / editors: Jacob Jefferson and Jennifer S. McGovern.
p. cm.
Includes index.
ISBN 978-1-62100-775-3 (softcover)
1. Broadcasting--Law and legislation--United States. 2. United States. Federal Communications Commission. 3.Obscenity (Law)--United States.4 United States.Constitution.1st Amendment. 5.Broadcasting policy--United States I.Jefferson, Jacob, 1969- II McGovern, Jennifer S(Jennifer Sharon), 1971-
KF2805.B77 2012
343.7309'94--dc23

2011038320

Published by Nova Science Publishers, Inc. † New York

CONTENTS

PREFACE

Federal law makes it a crime to utter "any obscene, indecent, or profane language by means of radio communication." Violators of this statute are subject to fines and imprisonment of up to two years, and the Federal Communication Commission (FCC) may enforce this provision by forfeiture or revocation of a broadcaster's license. Various federal officials have spoken in favor of extending the FCC's indecency restriction, which currently applies to broadcast television and radio, to cable and satellite television. This book examines whether such an extension would violate the First Amendment's guarantee of freedom of speech.

Chapter 1- Two prominent television events placed increased attention on the Federal Communications Commission (FCC) and the broadcast indecency statute that it enforces. The airing of an expletive by Bono during the 2003 Golden Globe Awards, as well as the "wardrobe malfunction" that occurred during the 2004 Super Bowl halftime show, gave broadcast indecency prominence in the 109th and 110th Congresses, and resulted in the enactment of P.L. 109-235 (2006), which increased the penalties for broadcast indecency by tenfold.

Federal law makes it a crime to utter "any obscene, indecent, or profane language by means of radio communication" (18 U.S.C. §1464). Violators of this statute are subject to fines and imprisonment of up to two years, and the FCC may enforce this provision by forfeiture or revocation of a broadcaster's license. The FCC has found that, for material to be "indecent," it "must describe or depict sexual or excretory organs or activities," and "must be patently offensive as measured by contemporary community standards for the broadcast medium." The federal government's authority to regulate material that is "indecent" but not obscene was upheld by the Supreme Court in

Federal Communications Commission v. Pacifica Foundation, which found that prohibiting such material during certain times of the day does not violate the First Amendment.

Chapter 2- Various federal officials have spoken in favor of extending the Federal Communication Commission's indecency restriction, which currently applies to broadcast television and radio, to cable and satellite television. This report examines whether such an extension would violate the First Amendment's guarantee of freedom of speech.

The FCC's indecency restriction was enacted pursuant to a federal statute that, insofar as it was found constitutional, requires the FCC to promulgate regulations to prohibit the broadcast of indecent programming from 6 a.m. to 10 p.m. The FCC has found that, for material to be "indecent," it "must describe or depict sexual or excretory organs or activities," and "must be patently offensive as measured by contemporary community standards for the broadcast medium."

Chapter 3- The Fairness Doctrine was a policy of the Federal Communications Commission (FCC or Commission) that required broadcast licensees to cover issues of public importance and to do so in a fair manner. Issues of public importance were not limited to political campaigns. Nuclear plant construction, workers' rights, and other issues of focus for a particular community could gain the status of an issue that broadcasters were required to cover. Therefore, the Fairness Doctrine was distinct from the so-called "equal time" rule, which requires broadcasters to grant equal time to qualified candidates for public office, because the Fairness Doctrine applied to a much broader range of topics.

In 1987, after a period of study, the FCC repealed the Fairness Doctrine. The FCC found that the doctrine likely violated the free speech rights of broadcasters, led to less speech about issues of public importance over broadcast airwaves, and was no longer required because of the increase in competition among mass media. The repeal of the doctrine did not end the debate among lawmakers, scholars, and others about its constitutionality and impact on the availability of diverse information to the public.

In: Broadcasting, the FCC, Indecency ... ISBN: 978-1-62100--775-3
Editors: J. Jefferson and J. McGovern

Chapter 1

REGULATION OF BROADCAST INDECENCY: BACKGROUND AND LEGAL ANALYSIS*

Kathleen Ann Ruane

SUMMARY

Two prominent television events placed increased attention on the Federal Communications Commission (FCC) and the broadcast indecency statute that it enforces. The airing of an expletive by Bono during the 2003 Golden Globe Awards, as well as the "wardrobe malfunction" that occurred during the 2004 Super Bowl halftime show, gave broadcast indecency prominence in the 109th and 110th Congresses, and resulted in the enactment of P.L. 109-235 (2006), which increased the penalties for broadcast indecency by tenfold.

Federal law makes it a crime to utter "any obscene, indecent, or profane language by means of radio communication" (18 U.S.C. §1464). Violators of this statute are subject to fines and imprisonment of up to two years, and the FCC may enforce this provision by forfeiture or revocation of a broadcaster's license. The FCC has found that, for material to be "indecent," it "must describe or depict sexual or excretory organs or activities," and "must be patently offensive as measured by contemporary community standards for the broadcast medium." The federal government's authority to regulate material that is "indecent" but

* This is an edited, reformatted and augmented version of a Congressional Research Service publication, CRS Report for Congress RL32222, from www.crs.gov, dated July 13, 2011.

not obscene was upheld by the Supreme Court in *Federal Communications Commission v. Pacifica Foundation*, which found that prohibiting such material during certain times of the day does not violate the First Amendment.

In 1992, Congress enacted P.L. 102-356 (47 U.S.C. §303 note), section 16(a) of which, as interpreted by the courts, requires the FCC to prohibit "indecent" material on broadcast radio and broadcast television from 6 a.m. to 10 p.m. Under P.L. 109-235, "indecent" broadcasts are now subject to a fine of up to "$325,000 for each violation or each day of continuing violation, except that the amount assessed for any continuing violation shall not exceed a total of $3,000,000 for any single act or failure to act." Fines may be levied against broadcast stations, but not against broadcast networks. The FCC appears to have the statutory authority to fine performers as well (up to $32,500 per incident), but has taken the position that "[c]ompliance with federal broadcast decency restrictions is the responsibility of the station that chooses to air the programming, not the performers."

The federal restriction on "indecent" material applies only to broadcast media, and this stems from the fact that there are a limited number of broadcast frequencies available and that the Supreme Court, therefore, allows the government to regulate broadcast media more than other media. This report discusses the legal evolution of the FCC's indecency regulations, and provides an overview of how the current regulations have been applied. The final section of the report considers whether prohibiting the broadcast of "indecent" words regardless of context would violate the First Amendment. This question arises because the Supreme Court in *Pacifica* left open the question whether broadcasting an occasional expletive, as in the Bono case, would justify a sanction.

INTRODUCTION

Two prominent television events placed increased attention on the Federal Communications Commission (FCC) and the broadcast indecency statute that it enforces.[1] The airing of an expletive by Bono during the 2003 Golden Globe Awards, as well as the "wardrobe malfunction" that occurred during the 2004 Super Bowl halftime show, gave broadcast indecency prominence in the 109th and 110th Congresses, and resulted in the enactment of P.L. 109-235 (2006), which increased the penalties for broadcast indecency by tenfold.

Federal law makes it a crime to utter "any obscene, indecent, or profane language by means of radio communication" (18 U.S.C. §1464). Violators of this statute are subject to fines and imprisonment of up to two years, and the

FCC may enforce this provision by forfeiture or revocation of a broadcaster's license. The FCC has found that, for material to be "indecent," it "must describe or depict sexual or excretory organs or activities," and "must be patently offensive as measured by contemporary community standards for the broad-cast medium." The federal government's authority to regulate material that is "indecent" but not obscene was upheld by the Supreme Court in *Federal Communications Commission v. Pacifica Foundation,* which found that prohibitting such material during certain times of the day does not violate the First Amendment.

In 1992, Congress enacted P.L. 102-356 (47 U.S.C. §303 note), section 16(a) of which, as interpreted by the courts, requires the FCC to prohibit "indecent" material on broadcast radio and broadcast television from 6 a.m. to 10 p.m. Under P.L. 109-235, "indecent" broadcasts are now subject to a fine of up to "$325,000 for each violation or each day of continuing violation, except that the amount assessed for any continuing violation shall not exceed a total of $3,000,000 for any single act or failure to act." Fines may be levied against broadcast stations, but not against broadcast networks. The FCC appears to have the statutory authority to fine performers as well (up to $32,500 per incident), but has taken the position that "[c]ompliance with federal broadcast decency restrictions is the responsibility of the station that chooses to air the programming, not the performers."

The federal restriction on "indecent" material applies only to broadcast media, and this stems from the fact that there are a limited number of broadcast frequencies available and that the Supreme Court, therefore, allows the government to regulate broadcast media more than other media. It appears likely that a court would find that to apply the FCC's indecency restriction to cable or satellite media would violate the First Amendment.[2]

This report discusses the evolution of the FCC's indecency regulations, provides an overview of how the current regulations have been applied, and examines indecency legislation that was introduced in the 110th Congress. (The bill that increased penalties is the only such legislation that was enacted.) The final section of this report considers whether prohibiting the broadcast of "indecent" words regardless of context would violate the First Amendment. This issue arises because the Supreme Court in *Pacifica* left open the question of whether broadcasting an occasional expletive, as in the Bono case, would justify a sanction.

BACKGROUND

On January 19, 2003, broadcast television stations in various parts of the country aired the Golden Globe Awards. During the awards, the singer Bono,[3] in response to winning an award, said, "this is really, really f[***]ing brilliant."[4] In response to this utterance, the FCC received over 230 complaints alleging that the program was obscene or indecent, and requesting that the commission impose sanctions on the licensees for the broadcast of the material in question.[5]

The Enforcement Bureau of the FCC issued a Memorandum Opinion and Order on October 3, 2003, denying the complaints and finding that the broadcast of the Golden Globe Awards including Bono's utterance did not violate federal restrictions regarding the broadcast of obscene and indecent material.[6] The bureau dismissed the complaints primarily because the language in question did not describe or depict sexual or excretory activities or organs. The bureau noted that while "the word 'f[***]ing' may be crude and offensive," it "did not describe sexual or excretory organs or activities. Rather, the performer used the word 'f[***]ing' as an adjective or expletive to emphasize an exclamation."[7] The bureau added that in similar circumstances it "found that offensive language used as an insult rather than as a description of sexual or excretory activity or organs is not within the scope of the commission's prohibition on indecent program content."[8]

The decision of the Enforcement Bureau was met with opposition from a number of organizations and Members of Congress, and an appeal was filed for review by the full commission. FCC Chairman Michael Powell asked the full commission to overturn the Enforcement Bureau's ruling.[9]

On March 18, 2004, the full commission issued a *Memorandum Opinion and Order* granting the application for review and reversing the Enforcement Bureau's earlier opinion.[10] The commission found that the broadcasts of the Golden Globe Awards violated 18 U.S.C. 1464, but declined to impose a forfeiture on the broadcast licensees because the order reverses Commission precedent regarding the broadcast of the "F-word." This decision is discussed in detail below.

On February 1, 2004, CBS aired Super Bowl XXXVIII, with a halftime show produced by the MTV network. The show included performers singing and dancing provocatively, and ended with the exposure of the breast of one female performer. The network received numerous complaints regarding the halftime performance, and FCC Chairman Michael Powell initiated a formal investigation into the incident.[11]

On September 22, 2004, the FCC released a *Notice of Apparent Liability for Forfeiture* finding that the airing of the Super Bowl halftime show "apparently violate[d] the federal restrictions regarding the broadcast of indecent material."[12] The *NAL* imposes a forfeiture in the aggregate amount of $550,000 on Viacom Inc., the licensee or ultimate parent of the licensees with regard to whom the complaint was filed.[13] On March 15, 2006, the FCC issued a *Forfeiture Order* imposing a mandatory forfeiture in the amount of $550,000 on CBS for the airing of the 2004 Super Bowl halftime show. CBS appealed to the U.S. Court of Appeals for the Third Circuit, which, in 2008, invalidated the fine, but, in 2009, the Third Circuit's decision was vacated by the Supreme Court.[14] This case is discussed in greater detail below.

EVOLUTION OF THE FCC'S INDECENCY REGULATIONS

Title 18 of the United States Code makes it unlawful to utter "any obscene, indecent, or profane language by means of radio communication."[15] Violators of this provision are subject to fines or imprisonment of up to two years. The Federal Communications Commission has the authority to enforce this provision by forfeiture or revocation of license.[16] The commission's authority to regulate material that is indecent, but not obscene, was upheld by the Supreme Court in *Federal Communications Commission v. Pacifica Foundation.*[17] In *Pacifica,* the Supreme Court affirmed the commission's order regarding the airing of comedian George Carlin's "Filthy Words" monologue.[18] In that order, the commission determined that the airing of the monologue, which contained certain words that "depicted sexual and excretory activities in a patently offensive manner," at a time "when children were undoubtedly in the audience" was indecent and prohibited by 18 U.S.C. §1464.[19] Pursuant to the Court's decision, whether any such material is "patently offensive" is determined by "contemporary community standards for the broadcast medium."[20] The Court noted that indecency is "largely a function of context—it cannot be judged in the abstract."[21]

The commission's order in the *Pacifica* case relied partially on a spectrum scarcity argument; that is, that there is a scarcity of spectrum space so the government must license the use of such space in the public interest, and partially on "principles analogous to those found in the law of nuisance."[22] The commission noted that public nuisance law generally aims to channel the offensive behavior rather than to prohibit it outright. For example, in the context of broadcast material, channeling would involve airing potentially offensive material at times when children are less likely to be in the audience. In 1987, the commission rejected the spectrum scarcity argument as a sufficient basis for its regulation of broadcast indecency, but noted that it would continue to rely upon the validity of the public nuisance rationale, including channeling of potentially objectionable material.[23] However, in its 1987 order, the commission also stated that channeling based on a specific time of day was no longer a sufficient means to ensure that children were not in the audience when indecent material aired and warned licensees that indecent material aired after 10 p.m. would be actionable.[24] The commission further clarified its earlier *Pacifica* order, noting that indecent language was not strictly limited to the seven words at issue in the original broadcast in question, and that repeated use of those words was not necessary to find that material in question was indecent.[25]

The commission's 1987 orders were challenged by parties alleging that the commission had changed its indecency standard and that the new standard was unconstitutional. In *Action for Children's Television v. Federal Communications Commission (ACT I)*, the United States Court of Appeals for the District of Columbia Circuit upheld the standard used by the commission to determine whether broadcast material was indecent, but it vacated the commission's order with respect to the channeling of indecent material for redetermination "after a full and fair hearing of the times at which indecent material may be broadcast."[26]

Following the court's decision in *Action for Children's Television (ACT I)*, a rider to the Commerce, Justice, State FY89 Appropriations Act required the FCC to promulgate regulations to ban indecent broadcasts 24 hours a day.[27] The commission followed the congressional mandate and promulgated regulations prohibiting all broadcasts of indecent material.[28] The new regulations were challenged, and the United States Court of Appeals for the District of Columbia Circuit vacated the commission's order.[29] In so doing, the court noted that in *ACT I* it held that the commission "must identify some reasonable period of time during which indecent material may be broadcast," thus precluding a ban on such broadcasts at all times.[30]

In 1992, Congress enacted the Public Telecommunications Act of 1992, which required the FCC to promulgate regulations to prohibit the broadcasting of indecent material from 6 a.m. to midnight, except for broadcasts by public radio and television stations that go off the air at or before midnight, in which case such stations may broadcast indecent material beginning at 10 p.m.[31] The commission promulgated regulations as mandated in the act.[32] The new regulations were challenged, and a three-judge panel of the United States

Court of Appeals for the District of Columbia Circuit subsequently vacated the commission's order implementing the act and held the underlying statute unconstitutional.[33] In its order implementing the act, the FCC set forth three goals to justify the regulations: (1) ensuring that parents have an opportunity to supervise their children's listening and viewing of over-the-air broadcasts; (2) ensuring the well being of minors regardless of supervision; and (3) protecting the right of all members of the public to be free of indecent material in the privacy of their homes.[34] The court rejected the third justification as "insufficient to support a restriction on the broadcasting of constitutionally protected indecent material," but accepted the first two as compelling interests.[35] Despite the finding of compelling interests in the first two, the court found that both Congress and the FCC had failed "to tailor their efforts to advance these interests in a sufficiently narrow way to meet constitutional standards."[36]

Following the decision of the three-judge panel, the commission requested a rehearing *en banc*.[37] The case was reheard on October 19, 1994, and, on June 30, 1995, the full court of appeals held the statute unconstitutional insofar as it prohibited the broadcast of indecent material between the hours of 10 p.m. and midnight on non-public stations.[38] In so doing, the court held that while the channeling of indecent broadcasts between midnight and 6 a.m. "would not unduly burden the First Amendment," the distinction drawn by Congress between public and non-public broadcasters "bears no apparent relationship to the compelling government interests that [the restrictions] are intended to serve."[39] The court remanded the regulations to the FCC with instructions to modify the regulations to permit the broadcast of indecent material on all stations between 10 p.m. and 6 a.m.

CURRENT REGULATIONS

Following the decision in *ACT III*, the commission modified its indecency regulations to prohibit indecent broadcasts from 6 a.m. to 10 p.m.[40] The modified regulations became effective August 28, 1995.[41] These regulations have been enforced primarily with respect to radio broadcasts and thus have been applied more often to indecent language rather than to images.[42] Under these regulations, broadcasts deemed indecent were subject to a forfeiture of up to $32,500 per violation,[43] with the FCC's considering each utterance of an indecent word as a separate violation, rather than viewing the entire program as a single violation.[44]

Fines may be levied against broadcast stations, but not against broadcast networks. The FCC appears also to have the statutory authority to fine performers for uttering indecent words,[45] but it has taken the position that "[c]ompliance with federal broadcast decency restrictions is the responsibility of the station that chooses to air the programming, not the performers."[46]

On June 15, 2006, the President signed S. 193, 109th Congress, into law, and it became P.L. 109- 235, the Broadcast Decency Enforcement Act of 2005. This law increased the penalty for indecent broadcasts tenfold, to $325,000 for each violation, with a maximum of $3 million "for any single act or failure to act." This increased penalty may be levied against "a broadcast station licensee or permittee; or an applicant for any broadcast license, permit, certificate, or other instrument or authorization issued by the Commission." If the FCC were to change its policy and impose fines on performers, it could apparently do so only under the provision (which remains in effect) that authorizes forfeitures of up to $32,500 per violation.[47]

To determine whether broadcast material is in fact indecent, the commission must make two fundamental determinations: (1) that the material alleged to be indecent falls within the subject matter scope of the definition of indecency—the material in question must describe or depict sexual or excretory organs or activities; and (2) that the broadcast is patently offensive as measured by contemporary community standards for the broadcast medium.[48] If the material in question does not fall within the subject matter scope of the indecency definition, or if the broadcast occurred during the "safe harbor" hours (between 10 p.m. and 6 a.m.), the complaint is usually dismissed. However, if the commission determines that the complaint meets the subject matter requirements and was aired outside the "safe harbor" hours, the broadcast in question is evaluated for patent offensiveness. The commission notes that in determining whether material is patently offensive, the full context is very important, and such determinations are highly fact-specific.

The commission has identified three factors that have significant in recent decisions in determining whether broadcast material is patently offensive:

> (1) the explicitness or graphic nature of the description or depiction of sexual or excretory organs or activities;
>
> (2) whether the material dwells on or repeats at length descriptions of sexual or excretory organs or activities;
>
> (3) whether the material appears to pander or is used to titillate, or whether the material appears to have been presented for its shock value.[49]

A discussion of cases that address each of these factors follows.

Explicitness or Graphic Nature of Material

Generally, the more explicit or graphic the description or depiction, the greater the likelihood that the material will be deemed patently offensive and therefore indecent. For example, the commission imposed a forfeiture on a university radio station for airing a rap song that included a line depicting anal intercourse.[50] In that case, the commission determined that the song described sexual activities in graphic terms that were patently offensive and therefore indecent. Since the song was broadcast in the mid-afternoon, there was a reasonable risk that children were in the audience, thus giving rise to the commission's action.[51]

Broadcasts need not be as graphic as the song in the above case to give rise to the imposition of an FCC forfeiture. Broadcasts consisting of double entendres or innuendos may also be deemed indecent if the "sexual or excretory import is unmistakable." The FCC issued a notice of apparent liability and imposed a forfeiture on several stations for airing a song that included the following lines: "I whipped out my Whopper and whispered, Hey, Sweettart, how'd you like to Crunch on my Big Hunk for a Million Dollar Bar? Well, she immediately went down on my Tootsie Roll and you know, it was like pure Almond Joy."[52] The commission determined that the material was indecent even though it used candy bar names to substitute for sexual activities. In one notice concerning the broadcast of the song, the commission stated that "[w]hile the passages arguably consist of double entendre and indirect references, the language used in each passage was understandable and clearly capable of specific sexual meaning and, because of the context, the sexual import was inescapable."[53] The nature of the lyrics, coupled with the fact that the song aired between 6 a.m. and 10 p.m., gave rise to the imposition of a forfeiture.

Dwelling or Repetition of Potentially Offensive Material

Repetition of and persistent focus on a sexual or excretory activity could "exacerbate the potential offensiveness of broadcasts." For example, the FCC issued a notice of apparent liability and imposed a forfeiture on a radio station that broadcast an extensive discussion of flatulence and defecation by radio personality "Bubba, the Love Sponge."[54] Though the broadcast did not contain any expletives, the commission found that the material dwelt on excretory activities and therefore was patently offensive.

While repetition can increase the likelihood that references to sexual or excretory activities are deemed indecent, where such references have been made in passing or are fleeting in nature, the commission has found that the reference was not indecent even when profanity has been used.[55] For example, the commission determined that the following phrase—"The hell I did, I drove mother-f[***]er, oh."—uttered by an announcer during a radio morning show, was not indecent.[56] The commission declined to take action regarding the broadcast because it contained only a "fleeting and isolated utterance ... within the context of live and spontaneous programming."[57] Certain fleeting references may, however, be found indecent where other factors contribute to the broadcast's patent offensiveness. For example, the commission has imposed forfeitures on stations for airing jokes that refer to sexual activities with children.[58]

Pandering or Titillating Nature of Material

In determining whether broadcast material is indecent, the commission also looks to the purpose for which the material is being presented. Indecency findings generally involve material that is presented in a pandering or titillating manner, or material that is presented for the shock value of its language. For example, the commission deemed a radio call-in survey about oral sex to be indecent based in part on the fact that the material was presented in a pandering and titillating manner.[59]

Whether a broadcast is presented in a pandering or titillating manner depends on the context in which the potentially indecent material is presented. Explicit images or graphic language does not necessarily mean that the broadcast is being presented in a pandering or titillating manner. For example, the commission declined to impose a forfeiture on a television station for airing portions of a high school sex education class that included the use of "sex organ models to demonstrate the use of various birth control devices."[60] In dismissing the complaint, the commission held that, "[a]lthough the program dealt with sexual issues, the material presented was clinical or instructional in nature and not presented in a pandering, titillating, or vulgar manner."[61]

Golden Globe Awards Decision

As noted above, on March 18, 2004, the Federal Communications Commission overturned an earlier decision by the commission's Enforcement Bureau regarding the broadcast of the word "f[***]ing" during the 2003 Golden Globe Awards. In the earlier decision, the Enforcement Bureau had found that the broadcast of the program including the utterance did not violate federal restrictions regarding the broadcast of obscene and indecent material.[62] The bureau dismissed the complaints primarily because the language in question did not describe or depict sexual or excretory activities or organs.

In its March 18 *Memorandum Opinion and Order*, the full commission concluded that the broadcast of the Golden Globe Awards did include material that violated prohibitions on the broadcast of indecent and profane material.[63] In reversing the bureau, the commission determined that the "phrase at issue is within the scope of our indecency definition because it does depict or describe sexual activities."[64] Although the commission "recognize[d] NBC's argument that the 'F-Word' here was used 'as an intensifier,'" it nevertheless concluded that, "given the core meaning of the 'F-Word,' any use of that word or a variation, in any context, inherently has a sexual connotation, and therefore falls within the first prong of our indecency definition."[65]

Upon finding that the phrase in question fell within the first prong of the definition of "indecency," the commission turned to the question of whether the broadcast was patently offensive under contemporary community standards for the broadcast medium. The commission determined that the broadcast was patently offensive, noting that "[t]he 'F-Word' is one of the most vulgar, graphic and explicit descriptions of sexual activity in the English language," and that "[t]he use of the 'F-Word' here, on a nationally telecast awards ceremony, was shocking and gratuitous."[66] The commission also rejected "prior Commission and staff action [that] have indicated that isolated or fleeting broadcasts of the 'F-Word' such as that here are not indecent or would not be acted upon," concluding "that any such interpretation is no longer good law."[67] The commission further clarified its position, stating "that the mere fact that specific words or phrases are not sustained or repeated does not mandate a finding that material that is otherwise patently offensive to the broadcast medium is not indecent."[68]

In addition to the determination that the utterance of the word "f[***]ing" during the Golden Globe Awards was indecent, the commission also found, as an independent ground for its decision, that use of the word was "profane" in violation of 18 U.S.C. 1464.[69] In making this determination, the commission cited dictionary definitions of "profanity" as "'vulgar, irreverent, or coarse language,'"[70] and a Seventh Circuit opinion stating that "profanity" is "'construable as denoting certain of those personally reviling epithets naturally tending to provoke violent resentment or denoting language so grossly offensive to members of the public who actually hear it as to amount to a nuisance.'"[71] The commission acknowledged that its limited case law regarding profane speech has focused on profanity in the context of blasphemy, but stated that it would no longer limit its definition of profane speech in such manner. Pursuant to its adoption of this new definition of "profane," the commission stated that, depending on the context, the "'F-Word' and those words (or variants thereof) that are as highly offensive as the 'F-Word'" would be considered "profane" if broadcast between 6 a.m. and 10 p.m.[72] The commission noted that other words would be considered on a case-by-case basis.

Super Bowl Halftime Show Decision

As noted above, on September 22, 2004, the FCC released a *Notice of Apparent Liability for Forfeiture* imposing a $550,000 forfeiture on several Viacom-owned CBS affiliates for the broadcast of the Super Bowl XXXVIII halftime show on February 1, 2004, in which a performer's breast was exposed.[73] The commission determined that the show, which was aired at approximately 8:30 p.m. Eastern Standard Time, violated its restrictions on the broadcast of indecent material.

In its analysis, the commission determined that since the broadcast included a performance that culminated in "on-camera partial nudity," and thus satisfied the first part of the indecency analysis, further scrutiny was warranted to determine whether the broadcast was "patently offensive as measured by contemporary community standards for the broadcast medium."[74] The commission found that the performance in question was "both explicit and graphic," and rejected the licensees' contention that since the exposure was fleeting, lasting only 19/32 of a second, it should not be deemed indecent.[75] In determining whether the material in question was intended to "pander to, titillate and shock the viewing audience," the commission noted that the performer's breast was exposed after another performer sang, "gonna have you naked by the end of this song."[76] The commission found that the song lyrics, coupled with simulated sexual activities during the performance and the exposure of the breast, indicated that the purpose of the performance was to pander to, titillate and shock the audience, and the fact that the actual exposure of the breast was brief, as noted above, was not dispositive.[77]

The commission ordered each Viacom-owned CBS affiliate to pay the statutory maximum forfeiture of $27,500 for the broadcast, for a total forfeiture of $550,000. The forfeiture was imposed on the Viacom-owned affiliates because of Viacom's participation in and planning of the Super Bowl halftime show with MTV networks, another Viacom subsidiary.[78]

Following the issuance of the *Notice of Apparent Liability for Forfeiture*, the affiliates are "afforded a reasonable period of time (usually 30 days from the date of the notice) to show, in writing, why a forfeiture penalty should not be imposed or should be reduced, or to pay the forfeiture."[79] CBS filed an opposition to the Notice of Apparent Liability on November 5, 2004. The opposition challenged the forfeiture on various grounds, including that the test for indecency was not met and that the forfeiture violates the First Amendment.

On March 15, 2006, the FCC issued a *Forfeiture Order* imposing a mandatory forfeiture in the amount of $550,000 on CBS for the airing of the 2004 Super Bowl halftime show.[80] CBS appealed to the U.S. Court of Appeals for the Third Circuit, which, on July 21, 2008, invalidated the fine, but, on May 4, 2009, the Supreme Court vacated the Third Circuit's decision.[81] The court's decision is discussed in greater detail below.

Other Recent Enforcement Actions

In addition to the *Order* regarding the 2004 Super Bowl halftime show, the FCC issued several *Notices of Apparent Liability* for various television broadcasts occurring between February 2, 2002, and March 8, 2005.[82]

Of the six programs for which a forfeiture was proposed, two of the complaints were based on the use of "indecent" language, two were based on sexually explicit images, and two programs were cited for both language and sexual innuendo.[83] In determining whether a forfeiture was appropriate, the commission applied the modified analysis first used in the *Golden Globe Awards Order* with respect to language that is deemed "indecent," and in the *Super Bowl Halftime Show Order* regarding sexually explicit imagery.[84]

In addition to the commission's recent actions with respect to televised programming, the commission had previously imposed forfeitures on a number of radio stations for broadcast indecency.[85] We now discuss two of its more recent high-profile actions related to radio programming. Each of these actions resulted in a consent decree between the commission and the broadcaster.

Infinity Broadcasting

On October 2, 2003, the commission issued a *Notice of Apparent Liability* to Infinity Broadcasting for airing portions of the "Opie & Anthony Show" during which the hosts conducted a contest entitled "Sex for Sam" which involved couples having sex in certain "risky" locations throughout New York City in an effort to win a trip.[86] The couples, accompanied by a station employee, were to have sex in as many of the designated locations as possible. They were assigned points based on the nature of the location and the activities in which they engaged. The station aired discussions between the hosts of the show and the station employee accompanying the couples which consisted of descriptions of the sexual activities of the participating couples and the locations in which they engaged in sexual activities. One discussion involved an description of a couple apparently engaging in sexual activities in St. Patrick's Cathedral.

The commission determined that the broadcast made "graphic and explicit references to sexual and excretory organs and activity" despite the fact that colloquial terms, rather than explicit or graphic terms, were used in the descriptions. The commission found that "[t]o the extent that the colloquial terms that the participants used to describe organs and activities could be described as innuendo rather than as direct references, they are nonetheless sufficient to render the material actionably indecent because the 'sexual [and] excretory import' of those references was 'unmistakable.'"[87] The commission also found that the hosts of the show "dwelled at length on and referred repeatedly to sexual or excretory activities and organs," and that "the descriptions of sexual and excretory activity and organs were not in any way isolated and fleeting."[88]

On November 23, 2004, the FCC entered into a consent decree with Infinity regarding the Opie & Anthony *NAL*.[89] Pursuant to the decree, Infinity, a subsidiary of Viacom, agreed to make a voluntary contribution to the United States Treasury in the amount of $3.5 million and to adopt a company-wide compliance plan for the purpose of preventing the broadcast of indecent material. As part of the company-wide plan, Viacom agreed to install delay systems to edit "potentially problematic" live programming and to conduct training with respect to indecency regulations for all of its on-air talent and employees who participate in programming decisions.

Clear Channel Broadcasting

On January 27, 2004, the commission issued a *Notice of Apparent Liability* to Clear Channel Broadcasting for repeated airings of the "Bubba, the Love Sponge" program which included indecent material.[90] The commission found that all the broadcasts in question involved "conversations about such things as oral sex, penises, testicles, masturbation, intercourse, orgasms and breasts."[91] The commission determined that each of the broadcasts in question contained "sufficiently graphic and explicit references," which were generally repeated throughout the broadcast in a pandering and titillating manner.

In one broadcast, the station aired a segment involving skits in which the voices of purported cartoon characters talk about drugs and sex.[92] The skits were inserted between advertisements for Cartoon Network's Friday-night cartoons. The commission determined that "the use of cartoon characters in such a sexually explicit manner during hours of the day when children are likely to be listening is shocking and makes this segment patently offensive."[93] The commission also cited the "calculated and callous nature of the stations' decision to impose this predictably offensive material upon young, vulnerable listeners" as "weighing heavily" in its determination.[94]

On April 8, 2004, the commission released another *Notice of Apparent Liability* against Clear Channel Communications for airing allegedly indecent material during the "Howard Stern Show."[95] For the first time, the commission sought to impose separate statutory maximum forfeitures for each indecent utterance during the program in question, rather than imposing a single fine for the entire program.[96]

The commission entered into a consent decree with Clear Channel on June 9, 2004. The decree requires Clear Channel to make a "voluntary contribution" of $1.75 million to the United States Treasury and outlines "a company-wide compliance plan for the purpose of preventing the broadcast over radio or television of material violative of the indecency laws."[97] As part of the compliance plan, Clear Channel will "conduct training on obscenity and indecency for all on-air talent and employees who materially participate in programming decisions, which will include tutorials regarding material that the FCC does not permit broadcasters to air."[98] The plan also requires Clear Channel to suspend any employee accused of airing, or who materially participates in the decision to air, obscene or indecent material while an investigation is conducted following the issuance of a *Notice of Apparent Liability*. Such employees will be terminated without delay if the *NAL* results in enforcement action by the FCC.

RECENT SUPREME COURT AND APPEALS COURT DECISIONS

Two major cases were decided by federal courts of appeals in 2007 and 2008. Both cases invalidated forfeiture orders the FCC had issued against broadcasters for transmitting fleeting indecent material over the airwaves. In April of 2009, the Supreme Court overturned the decision of the appeals court in the first case and remanded the case to the Second Circuit for proceedings consistent with the Supreme Court's opinion. The Supreme Court also ordered the decision in the second case to be reconsidered by the Third Circuit. Upon reconsideration, the Second Circuit struck down the FCC's indecency policy for violating the First Amendment. The FCC has appealed that decision to the Supreme Court.

Fox Television Stations, Inc. v. FCC (Supreme Court Decision)

The FCC had taken action against, among other broadcasts, two award shows, described in an Associated Press article as, "a December 9, 2002, broadcast of the Billboard Music Awards in which singer Cher used the phrase, 'F--- 'em,' and a December 10, 2003, Billboard awards show in which reality show star Nicole Richie said: 'Have you ever tried to get cow s--- out of a Prada purse? It's not so f--- simple.'"[99] These incidents raised the same questions that the FCC's action against the Bono expletive raised: whether a fleeting isolated expletive is "indecent" under federal law, and, if so, whether the First Amendment permits the FCC to enforce the law by punishing broadcasters for such utterances.

On June 4, 2007, the U.S. Court of Appeals for the Second Circuit, in a 2-1 decision, found "that the FCC's new policy regarding 'fleeting expletives' represent[ed] a significant departure from positions previously taken by the agency and relied on by the broadcast industry."[100] The court further found "that the FCC ha[d] failed to articulate a reasoned basis for this change in policy. Accordingly, [the court held] that the FCC's new policy regarding 'fleeting expletives' [was] arbitrary and capricious under the Administrative Procedure Act."[101] Having overturned the FCC policy on statutory grounds, the court had no occasion to decide whether it also violated the First Amendment. It explained, however, why it was "skeptical that the Commission can provide a reasonable explanation for its 'fleeting expletive' regime that would pass constitutional muster."[102] The final section of this report examines this aspect of the court's opinion.

On April 28, 2009, the Supreme Court, in a 5-4 ruling, overturned the decision of the Second Circuit.[103] The Court found that the policy shift of the FCC was "entirely rational."[104] The Court found that the Second Circuit had relied on an erroneous interpretation of Supreme Court precedent when measuring the adequacy of the FCC's reasoning for its policy shift. According to the Court, the Second Circuit had applied a heightened standard of review to agency decisions that effect changes in prior policy. The Second Circuit interpreted that Supreme Court precedent to require the agency to articulate "why the new rule effectuates the statute as well or better than the old rule."[105]

The Supreme Court found no basis in its precedent or in the Administrative Procedure Act for such a requirement. The Court explained that the opinion upon which the Second Circuit had relied did not require agencies to articulate reasons for policy changes that were more substantial than those required to adopt a policy in the first instance. The precedent held, rather, that new actions required "a reasoned analysis for the change beyond that which may be required when an agency *does not act* in the first instance."[106] The FCC need not have demonstrated that the reasons for its new policies were better than the reasons for the old one. It was sufficient for the agency to show that the new policy is permissible under the statute; there are good reasons for it; and the agency believes it to be better, "which the conscious change of course adequately indicates."[107]

Applying this standard to the FCC's rule change, the Court found that the FCC's actions were not arbitrary or capricious. The FCC acknowledged that its actions represented a shift from prior policy. The Court also found the agency's reasons for its policy change were "entirely rational," because it was not unreasonable to treat literal and nonliteral uses of expletives in the same way. It was also reasonable, in the Court's estimation, to find even isolated utterances to fit within the definition of indecency. As a result, the Court upheld the FCC's new policy on enforcement of "fleeting expletives." The Court, however, declined to rule on the constitutionality of the policy.[108]

Regarding the issue of constitutionality, the Court noted the dicta of the Second Circuit. The Second Circuit, having overturned the FCC policy on statutory grounds, had no occasion to decide whether it also violated the First Amendment. In dicta, however, it explained why it was "skeptical that the Commission can provide a reasonable explanation for its 'fleeting expletive' regime that would pass constitutional muster."[109]

The court wrote that it was

> sympathetic to the Networks' contention that the FCC's indecency test is undefined, indiscernible, inconsistent, and consequently, unconstitutionally vague.... We also note that the FCC's indecency test raises the separate constitutional question of whether it permits the FCC to sanction speech based on its subjective view of the merit of that speech. It appears that under the FCC's current indecency regime, any and all uses of an expletive is presumptively indecent and profane with the broadcaster then having to demonstrate to the satisfaction of the Commission, under an unidentified burden of proof, that the expletives were "integral" to the work. In the licensing context, the Supreme Court has cautioned against speech regulations that give too much discretion to government officials.... Finally, we recognize that there is some tension in the law regarding the appropriate level of First Amendment scrutiny. In general, restrictions on First Amendment liberties prompt courts to apply strict scrutiny.... At the same time, however, the Supreme Court has also considered broadcast media exceptional.... Nevertheless, we would be remiss not to observe that it is increasingly difficult to describe the broadcast media as uniquely pervasive and uniquely accessible to children, and at some point in the future, strict scrutiny may properly apply in the context of regulating broadcast television.[110]

With respect to the Second Circuit's dicta regarding the First Amendment question, the Supreme Court wrote,

> It is conceivable that the Commission's orders may cause some broadcasters to avoid certain language that is beyond the Commission's reach under the Constitution. Whether that is so, and, if so, whether it is unconstitutional, will be determined soon enough, perhaps in this very case. Meanwhile, any chilled references to excretory and sexual material "surely lie at the periphery of First Amendment concern," Pacifica, 438 U.S., at 743 (plurality opinion of Stevens, J.). We see no reason to abandon our usual procedures in a rush to judgment without a lower court opinion. We decline to address the constitutional questions at this time.[111]

On July 13, 2010, the Second Circuit, as discussed below, invalidated the FCC's policy because the court determined it to be unconstitutionally vague.[112]

CBS Corp. v. FCC

On July 21, 2008, the U.S. Court of Appeals for the Third Circuit issued a unanimous decision to invalidate the FCC's fine against CBS broadcasting station affiliates for the broadcast of the Super Bowl Halftime Show that included a brief instance of partial nudity.[113] The court decided to invalidate the fine because the FCC had acted arbitrarily and capriciously when finding that the brief nudity was actionably indecent.

In its review of the FCC's previous actions in this area, the court noted that the FCC has the power to regulate indecency over the broadcast airwaves, but for much of the FCC's history the agency maintained an exception for fleeting instances of indecency.[114] The commission argued that its policy exempting fleeting instances of indecency over broadcast from enforcement applied only to fleeting indecent language and not to images.[115] The FCC claimed that fleeting indecent images had always been subject to enforcement; therefore, there was no departure from the FCC's previous approach to sanctions regarding such images. As a result, the FCC argued that the agency did not have to articulate a reasoned basis for its shift in policy, and it provided none.

The court examined the FCC's claim that the agency had previously made the distinction between images and language and that indecent fleeting images had always been subject to FCC enforcement.[116] The court found those claims to be unfounded. In its review of the FCC's previous decisions, the court could find no distinction between the way the agency treated fleeting indecent language as opposed to indecent images.[117] The court cited instances in which the FCC declined to issue fines for fleeting indecent images. In declining to institute enforcement actions, the agency had stated that the images were fleeting and covered by its policy of nonenforcement.[118] The court decided, on that basis, that the FCC's decision to consider the fleeting indecent image broadcast during the Halftime Show to be actionable was a shift in the FCC's policy towards the enforcement against such images.

Because the agency had decided to implement a policy shift, the agency was required to articulate a reasoned basis for doing so in order for the departure to be valid under the Administrative Procedure Act.[119] As noted above, the FCC argued that its policy toward fleeting indecent images had not changed. Consequently, the FCC articulated no reason for the shift in policy identified by the court of appeals. Because the FCC provided no basis for its departure from previous enforcement practices, the court held that the deviation from the prior policy of restraining from enforcement against fleeting images was arbitrary and capricious to the extent that it violated the APA.[120] The fine, therefore, could not be imposed on CBS for two reasons. First, the underlying policy shift was invalid, having no reasoned basis. Second, even if the policy had a reasoned basis, the enforcement action against CBS represented the first time that the FCC had articulated its intention to take action against fleeting indecent images (assuming, as the commission argued, that it had not done so in its *Golden Globes* decision). The new policy could not be applied retroactively to fine CBS in this case.[121] The court did not consider whether a policy punishing fleeting indecent images over broadcast television would violate the First Amendment.

The FCC petitioned the Supreme Court for certiorari.[122] On May 4, 2009, the Court granted the petition, vacated the judgment, and remanded the case to the Third Circuit for further consideration in light of the Supreme Court's decision in *FCC v. Fox Television Stations, Inc.*[123]

Fox Television v. FCC (Second Circuit)

As a result of the Supreme Court's decision in *FCC v. Fox Television*, described above, the case was remanded to the Second Circuit Court of Appeals for consideration of whether the FCC's indecency policy violated the First Amendment.[124] On July 13, 2010, a three-judge panel struck down the FCC's indecency policy because the court determined it to be unconstitutionally vague. The panel noted that a law is impermissibly vague "if it does not 'give the person of ordinary intelligence a reasonable opportunity to know what is prohibited."[125] While the vagueness doctrine does not require perfect clarity, it requires the law to give persons notice of what is prohibited and what is not. The panel found that the FCC's policy lacked such notice because it was impossible to determine what the FCC would find to be 'patently offensive' prior to broadcast, and the application of the exceptions to the FCC's presumptive prohibitions on two particular expletives were equally difficult to predict.

The court reached this conclusion by surveying the FCC's enforcement of its indecency policy, since its amendments of the policy in 2001. The court lists a number of instances, occasionally within the same program, where some words that referred to sexual organs or excretion were patently offensive (bull***t), and other words the referred to sexual organs or excretion were not (d**k and d***head).[126] In surveying the orders determining which expletives were permissible, the court could find no explanation offered by the FCC for why certain words were impermissibly indecent, while others were not.

The FCC argued that because it could not anticipate what broadcasters would say prior to broadcast, flexibility was necessary to determine what was indecent after the fact.[127] The court, however, seemed to find this argument to contribute to its finding that the policy was impermissibly vague. "If the FCC cannot anticipate what is indecent under its policy, it can hardly expect broadcasters to do so," the court found.[128]

Even where the policy stated a presumptive violation of the indecency policy, the court found the policy to be vague.[129] The FCC has a presumptive prohibition on the use of the words "f***" and "sh**" outside of the safe harbor; however, there are two exceptions: the bona fide news exception and the artistic necessity exception. The court found it difficult to discern when either exception applied. For example, the use of these words in a broadcast of the fictional movie, *Saving Private Ryan*, did not violate the FCC's indecency policy because they fell under the artistic necessity exception. However, the use of these same words in the documentary "The Blues" did violate the policy and did not qualify for the exception. The court asked "how fleeting expletives could be more essential to the 'realism' of a fictional movie than to the 'realism' of interviews with real people about real life events."[130] The court continued, stating "it is hard not to speculate that the FCC simply was more comfortable with the themes in" *Saving Private Ryan*, raising the specter of censorship concerns.[131] The court avoided accusing the FCC of suppressing particular viewpoints, but noted that "nothing would prevent the FCC from applying its indecency policy in a discriminatory manner in the future."[132] The court also pointed out inconsistent applications of the bona fide news exception. The court cited an instance wherein the FCC found the use of one of the presumptively prohibited words to be indecent because it was uttered during a morning news program, only for the FCC to reverse its decision and find that the use of the word was not indecent *because it was used during a morning news program*.[133]

The panel noted that the FCC's policy had a significant chilling effect on the speech of broadcasters and noted a number of programs that broadcasters had refused to air for fear of violating the policy. "By prohibiting all 'patently offensive' references to sex, sexual organs, and excretion without giving adequate guidance as to what 'patently offensive' means, the FCC effectively chills speech, because broadcasters have no way of knowing what the FCC will find offensive."[134] Thus the court struck down the policy.

Notably, the court did not decide whether it was unconstitutional to punish "fleeting expletives" or single uses of an indecent word or image. Instead, the court invalidated the FCC's entire indecency policy as impermissibly vague, a broader decision than might have been expected under the facts of the case.

Current Status

The Supreme Court has agreed to review the decision of the Second Circuit, striking down the FCC's policy as a violation of the First Amendment.[135] Justice Thomas, in his concurring opinion in *Fox Television Stations, Inc. v. FCC*, indicated that he would be open to considering whether a rule that punishes the single occurrence of indecency is constitutional.[136] The Third Circuit has yet to render its decision on the constitutionality of the FCC's indecency policy in *CBS v. FCC*.

Would Prohibiting the Broadcast of "Indecent" Words Regardless of Context Violate the First Amendment?

Prior to striking down the FCC's most recent indecency policy for vagueness, the Second Circuit analyzed the continued vitality of the Supreme Court's 1978 broadcast indecency case, *Federal Communications Commission v. Pacifica*. In that case, the Supreme Court upheld, against a First Amendment challenge, an action that the FCC took against a radio station for broadcasting a recording of George Carlin's "Filthy Words" monologue at 2 p.m.[137] The Court has not decided a case on the issue of "indecent" speech on broadcast radio or television since then, but it did cite *Pacifica* with approval in 1997, when, in *Reno v. ACLU*, it contrasted regulation of the broadcast media with regulation of the Internet.[138] Nevertheless, the Court in *Reno* did not *hold* that *Pacifica* remains good law, and arguments have been made that the proliferation of cable television channels has rendered archaic *Pacifica*'s denial of full First Amendment rights to broadcast media.

In its most recent opinion in *Fox Television v. FCC*, the Second Circuit questioned the continued application of a special First Amendment standard to broadcasters.[139] One of the original justifications for the lowered broadcast free speech standard was the unique position of broadcast in the United States' media landscape. Broadcast was, according to the *Pacifica* Court, "uniquely accessible to children" and "uniquely pervasive in the lives of all Americans."[140] The Second Circuit found that the same cannot be said today.[141] With the ubiquity of cable, satellite, and the Internet, the Second Circuit found it difficult to hold that broadcasting remains uniquely pervasive. The Second Circuit also pointed out that blocking and filtering technology for broadcasts, like the V-chip, may provide a less restrictive means for managing indecent content over broadcast than the sanctions upheld in *Pacifica* and enforced by the FCC.[142] Nonetheless, the Second Circuit recognized that *Pacifica* remained controlling precedent and applied the standard set forth by the Supreme Court in that case.

Even if *Pacifica* remains valid, *Pacifica* did not hold that the First Amendment permits the ban either of an occasional expletive on broadcast media, or of programs that would not be likely to attract youthful audiences, even if such programs contain "indecent" language. On these points, Justice Stevens wrote for the Court in *Pacifica*:

> It is appropriate, in conclusion, to emphasize the narrowness of our holding. This case does not involve a two-way radio conversation between a cab driver and a dispatcher, or a telecast of an Elizabethan comedy. We have not decided that an occasional expletive in either setting would justify any sanction.... The time of day was emphasized by the Commission. The content of the program in which the language is used will also affect the composition of the audience.[143]

In a footnote to the last sentence of this quotation, the Court added: "Even a prime-time recitation of Geoffrey Chaucer's Miller's Tale would not be likely to command the attention of many children."[144] At the same time, Justice Stevens acknowledged that the Carlin monologue has political content: "The monologue does present a point of view; it attempts to show that the words it uses are 'harmless' and that our attitudes toward them are 'essentially silly.' The Commission objects, [however,] not to this point of view, but to the way in which it is expressed."[145] The Court commented: "If there were any reason to believe that the Commission's characterization of the Carlin monologue as offensive could be traced to its political content—or even to the fact that it satirized contemporary attitudes about four-letter words—First Amendment protection might be required."[146]

There appears to be some tension between this comment and the Court's remark about Chaucer, as any attempt to censor Chaucer would presumably also be based not on its ideas but on the way its ideas are expressed. But, as noted above, the Court's remark about Chaucer was a footnote to its comment that "[t]he content of the program in which the language is used will also affect the composition of the audience." Therefore, the difference that Justice Stevens apparently perceived between Chaucer and Carlin was that, even if both have literary, artistic, or political value, only the latter would be likely to attract a youthful audience. Arguably, then, *Pacifica* would permit the censorship, during certain hours, of the broadcast even of works of art that are likely to attract a youthful audience.[147]

If so, this would be contrary to the Court's opposition, in other contexts, to the censorship of works of art. The Court has held that even "materials [that] depict or describe patently offensive 'hard core' sexual conduct," which would otherwise be obscene, may not be prohibited if they have "serious literary, artistic, political, or scientific value."[148] In addition, the "harmful to minors" statutes of the sort that the Supreme Court upheld in *Ginsberg v. New York* generally define "harmful to minors" to parallel the Supreme Court's definition of "obscenity," and thus prohibit distributing to minors only material that lacks serious value for minors.[149] This suggests that, if the FCC or Congress prohibited the broadcast during certain hours of "indecent" words regardless of context, the Court might be troubled by the prohibition's application to works with serious value, even though *Pacifica* allowed the censorship of Carlin's monologue, despite its apparently having serious value.

Yet, Justice Stevens noted a distinction in *Pacifica* between a point of view and the way in which it is expressed, and, though a majority of the justices did not join the part of the opinion that drew this distinction, a majority of the justices, by concurring in *Pacifica*'s holding, indicated that the political (or literary or artistic) content of Carlin's monologue did not prevent its censorship during certain hours on broadcast radio and television. Therefore, it appears that, in deciding the constitutionality of an FCC or a congressional action prohibiting the broadcasting, during certain hours, of material with "indecent" words, the Court might be troubled by its application to works with serious value only if those works would, like Chaucer's, not be likely to attract a substantial youthful audience.

In sum, the Court did not hold that the FCC could prohibit an occasional expletive, and did not hold that the FCC could prohibit offensive words in programs—even prime-time programs—that children would be unlikely to watch or listen to. The Court did not hold that the FCC could *not* take these actions, as the question whether it could was not before the Court. But the Court's language quoted above renders *Pacifica* of uncertain precedential value in deciding whether a ban, during certain hours, on the broadcast of "indecent" words regardless of context would be constitutional.

In the "Filthy Words" monologue, as the Supreme Court described it, George Carlin "began by referring to his thoughts about 'the words you couldn't say on the public, ah, airwaves, um, the ones you definitely wouldn't say, ever.' He proceeded to list those words and repeat them over and over in a variety of colloquialisms." The FCC, at the time, used essentially the same standard for "indecent" that it uses today: "[T]he concept of 'indecent' is intimately connected with the exposure of children to language that describes, in terms patently offensive as measured by contemporary community standards for the broadcast medium, sexual or excretory activities and organs."[150]

Most of Carlin's uses of the "filthy words," it appears from reading his monologue, which is included as an appendix to the Court's opinion, seem designed to show the words' multiple uses, apart from describing sexual or excretory activities or organs. Nevertheless, "the Commission concluded that certain words depicted sexual or excretory activities in a patently offensive manner."[151] Therefore, one might argue that, even if, under *Pacifica*, the First Amendment does not protect, during certain hours, the use on broadcast media of words that depict sexual or excretory activities in a patently offensive manner, it nevertheless might protect the use of those same words "as an adjective or expletive to emphasize an exclamation" (to quote the FCC Enforcement Bureau's opinion in the Bono case).

A counterargument might be that, in *Pacifica*, the Court noted that "the normal definition of 'indecent' merely refers to nonconformance with accepted standards of morality."[152] This suggests the possibility that the Court would have ruled the same way in *Pacifica* if the FCC had defined "indecent" loosely enough to include the use of a patently offensive word "as an adjective or expletive to emphasize an exclamation." But this is speculative, as the Court did not so rule. Further, as noted above, Court emphasized the narrowness of its holding, noting that it had "not decided that an occasional expletive ... would justify any sanction."

On what basis did the Court in *Pacifica* find that the FCC's action did not violate the First Amendment? In Part IV-C of opinion, which was joined by a majority of the justices, Justice Stevens wrote:

> [O]f all forms of communication, it is broadcasting that has received the most limited First Amendment protection. Thus, although other speakers cannot be licensed except under laws that carefully define and narrow official discretion, a broadcaster may be deprived of his license and his forum if the Commission decides that such an action would serve "the public interest, convenience, and necessity." Similarly, although the First Amendment protects newspaper publishers from being required to print the replies of those whom they criticize,
>
> Miami Herald Publishing Co. v. Tornillo, 418 U.S. 241, it affords no such protection to broadcasters; on the contrary, they must give free time to the victims of their criticism. Red Lion Broadcasting Co. v. FCC, 395 U.S. 367.
>
> The reasons for these distinctions are complex, but two have relevance to the present case. First, the broadcast media have established a uniquely pervasive presence in the lives of all Americans. Patently offensive, indecent material presented over the airwaves confronts the citizen, not only in public, but in the privacy of the home, where the individual's right to be left alone plainly outweighs the First Amendment rights of an intruder. Rowan v. Post Office Dept., 397 U.S. 728.... To say that one may avoid further offense by turning off the radio when he hears indecent language is like saying that the remedy for an assault is to run away after the first blow.
>
> Second, broadcasting is uniquely accessible to children, even those too young to read....Bookstores and motion picture theaters ... may be prohibited from making indecent material available to children. We held in Ginsberg v. New York, 390 U.S. 629, that the government's interest in the "well-being of its youth" and in supporting "parents' claim to authority in their own household" justified the regulation of otherwise protected expression.153

In sum, the Court held that, on broadcast radio and television, during certain times of day, certain material may be prohibited because (1) it is patently offensive and indecent, and (2) it threatens the well-being of minors and their parents' authority in their own household. This raises the question of the extent to which the Court continues to allow the government (1) to treat broadcast media differently from other media, and (2) to censor speech on the ground that it is patently offensive and indecent, or threatens the well-being of minors and their parents' authority in their own household.

Broadcast Media

In *Red Lion Broadcasting Co. v. FCC*, which the Court cited in the above quotation from *Pacifica*, the Court upheld the FCC's "fairness doctrine," which "imposed on radio and television broadcasters the requirement that discussion of public issues be presented on broadcast stations, and that each side of those issues must be given fair coverage."[154] The reason that the Court upheld the imposition of the fairness doctrine on broadcast media, though it would not uphold its imposition on print media, is that "[w]here there are substantially more individuals who want to broadcast than there are frequencies to allocate, it is idle to posit an unabridgeable First Amendment right to broadcast comparable to the right of every individual to speak, write, or publish."[155] "Licenses to broadcast," the Court added, "do not confer ownership of designated frequencies, but only the temporary privilege of using them. 47 U.S.C. §301. Unless renewed, they expire within three years. 47 U.S.C. §307(d). The statute mandates the issuance of licenses if the 'public convenience, interest, or necessity will be served thereby.' 47 U.S.C. §307(a)."[156]

The Court in *Red Lion* then noted:

> It is argued that even if at one time the lack of available frequencies for all who wished to use them justified the Government's choice of those who would best serve the public interest ... this condition no longer prevails so that continuing control is not justified. To this there are several answers. Scarcity is not entirely a thing of the past.[157]

With the plethora of cable channels today, has spectrum scarcity now become a thing of the past?

In *Turner Broadcasting System, Inc. v. FCC*, the Court held that the scarcity rationale does not apply to cable television:

> [C]able television does not suffer from the inherent limitations that characterize the broadcast medium.... [S]oon there may be no practical limitation on the number of speakers who may use the cable medium. Nor is there any danger of physical interference between two cable speakers attempting to use the same channel. In light of these fundamental technological differences between broadcast and cable transmission, application of a more relaxed standard of scrutiny adopted in Red Lion and the other broadcast cases is inapt when determining the First Amendment validity of cable regulation.[158]

One might argue that, if the scarcity rationale does not apply to cable television, then it should not apply to broadcast television either, because a person who because of scarcity cannot start a broadcast channel can start a cable channel.[159] But the Court has not ruled on the question; in *Turner* it wrote: "Although courts and commentators have criticized the scarcity rationale since its inception, we have declined to question its continuing validity as support for our broadcast jurisprudence, and see no reason to do so here."[160]

In 1987, however, the FCC abolished the fairness doctrine, on First Amendment grounds, noting that technological developments and advancements in the telecommunications marketplace have provided a basis for the Supreme Court to reconsider its holding in *Red Lion*. The FCC's decision was upheld by the U.S. Court of Appeals for the District of Columbia, and the Supreme Court declined to review the case.[161] The court of appeals did not rule on constitutional grounds, but rather concluded "that the FCC's decision that the fairness doctrine no longer served the public interest was neither arbitrary, capricious nor an abuse of discretion, and [we] are convinced that it would have acted on that finding to terminate the doctrine even in the absence of its belief that the doctrine was no longer constitutional."[162]

But, whether or not spectrum scarcity has become a thing of the past, it apparently would not today justify governmental restrictions on "indecent" speech. This is because, subsequent to the Court in *Turner* declining to question the applicability of the scarcity rationale to broadcast media, a plurality of justices noted, in *Denver Area Educational Telecommunications Consortium, Inc. v. FCC*, that, though spectrum scarcity continued to justify the "structural regulations at issue there [in *Turner*] (the 'must carry' rules), it has little to do with a case that involves the effects of television viewing on children. Those effects are the result of how parents and children view television programming, and how pervasive and intrusive that programming is. In that respect, cable and broadcast television differ little, if at all."[163] The plurality therefore upheld a federal statute that permits cable operators to prohibit indecent material on leased access channels. Thus, it appears that the Court today would not cite spectrum scarcity to justify restrictions on "indecent" material on broadcast media, but it might cite broadcast media's pervasiveness and intrusiveness.

Subsequent to *Denver Area*, in *United States v. Playboy Entertainment Group, Inc.*, the Court held that cable television has full First Amendment protection; that is, content-based restrictions on cable television receive strict scrutiny.[164] Thus, if, as the Court said in *Denver Area*, cable and broadcast media differ little, if at all, with respect to the regulation of "indecent" material, and, if, as the Court said in *Playboy*, cable television receives strict scrutiny, then, arguably, broadcast media would also receive strict scrutiny with regard to restrictions on "indecent" material.[165] It is possible, however, that, if cable and broadcast media differ little, then the Court might apply *Pacifica* to both broadcast and cable, rather than to neither.[166]

As noted above, the Second Circuit questioned the continued vitality of *Pacifica* in its most recent *Fox Television* decision.[167] Justice Thomas also indicated a willingness to reconsider the special lower First Amendment standard applied to broadcasters in his concurrence in the Supreme Court's *Fox Television* decision.[168] It is possible, therefore, that the Supreme Court might be poised to take up the question of the First Amendment standard that should be applied to broadcasters in the near future. In any event, even if the Court were to continue to apply *Pacifica* to restrictions on broadcast media, this does not necessarily mean that it would uphold a ban on the broadcast of "indecent" language regardless of context, as *Pacifica* did not hold that an occasional expletive would justify a sanction.

Strict Scrutiny

What analysis might the Court apply in deciding the constitutionality of a ban on the broadcast of "indecent" language regardless of context? The Court in *Pacifica*, as noted, offered two reasons why the FCC could prohibit offensive speech on broadcast media: "First, the broadcast media have established a uniquely pervasive presence in the lives of all Americans. Patently offensive, indecent material presented over the airwaves confronts the citizen, not only in public, but in the privacy of the home.... Second, broadcasting is uniquely accessible to children, even those too young to read," and the government has an interest in the "well-being of its youth" and "in supporting 'parents' claim to authority in their own household.'" The first of these reasons apparently refers to adults as well as to children.

Ordinarily, when the government restricts speech, including "indecent" speech, on the basis of its content, the restriction, if challenged, will be found constitutional only if it satisfies "strict scrutiny."[169] This means that the government must prove that the restriction serves "to promote a compelling interest" and is "the least restrictive means to further the articulated interest."[170] The Court in *Pacifica* did not apply this test or any weaker First Amendment test, and did not explain why it did not. Its reason presumably was that the FCC's action restricted speech only on broadcast media. If, however, the Court were not to apply *Pacifica* in determining the constitutionality of a ban, during certain hours, on the broadcast of "indecent" language regardless of context, then it would apparently apply strict scrutiny.

If the Court were to apply strict scrutiny in making this determination, it seems unlikely that it would find the first reason cited in *Pacifica*—sparing citizens, including adults, from patently offensive or indecent words—to constitute a compelling governmental interest. The Court has held that the government may not prohibit the use of offensive words unless they "fall within [a] relatively few categories of instances," such as obscenity, fighting words, or words "thrust upon unwilling or unsuspecting viewers."[171]

If the Court were to apply strict scrutiny in determining the constitutionality of a ban, during certain hours, on the broadcast of "indecent" language regardless of context, it also might not find the second reason cited in *Pacifica*—protecting minors from patently offensive and indecent words and "supporting 'parents' claim to authority in their own household'"—to constitute a compelling governmental interest. When the Court considers the constitutionality of a restriction on speech, it ordinarily—even when the speech lacks full First Amendment protection and the court applies less than strict scrutiny—requires the government to "demonstrate that the recited harms are real, not merely conjectural, and that the regulation will in fact alleviate these harms in a direct and material way."[172] With respect to restrictions designed to deny minors access to sexually explicit material, by contrast, the courts appear to assume, without requiring evidence, that such material is harmful to minors, or to consider it "obscene as to minors," even if it is not obscene as to adults, and therefore not entitled to First Amendment protection with respect to minors, whether it is harmful to them or not.[173] In another case, a federal court of appeals, upholding the current statute that bans "indecent" broadcasts from 6 a.m. to 10 p.m., noted

> that the Supreme Court has recognized that the Government's interest in protecting children extends beyond shielding them from physical and psychological harm. The statute that the Court found constitutional in Ginsberg sought to protect children from exposure to materials that would "impair [their] ethical and moral development.... Congress does not need the testimony of psychiatrists and social scientists in order to take note of the coarsening of impressionable minds that can result from a persistent exposure to sexually explicit material."

Action for Children's Television v. FCC, *supra*, 58 F.3d at 662 (brackets and italics supplied by the court). A dissenting judge in the case noted that, "[t]here is not one iota of evidence in the record ... to support the claim that exposure to indecency is harmful—indeed, the nature of the alleged 'harm' is never explained." *Id.* at 671 (D.C. Cir. 1995) (Edwards, C.J., dissenting). A word used as a mere adjective or expletive, however, arguably does not constitute sexually oriented material.[174] Therefore, if a court applied strict scrutiny to decide the constitutionality of a ban, during certain hours, on the broadcast of "indecent" words regardless of context, then, in determining the presence of a compelling interest, the court might require the government to "demonstrate that the recited harms are real, not merely conjectural, and that the regulation will in fact alleviate these harms in a direct and material way." This could raise the question, not raised in *Pacifica*, of whether hearing such words is harmful to minors. More precisely, it might raise the question of whether hearing such words on broadcast radio and television is harmful to minors, even in light of the opportunities for minors to hear such words elsewhere. If the government failed to prove that hearing certain words on broadcast radio or television is harmful to minors, then a court would not find a compelling interest in censoring those words and might strike down the law.

It might still uphold the law, however, if it found that the law served the government's interest "in supporting 'parents' claim to authority in their own household,'" and that this is a compelling interest independent from the interest in protecting the well-being of minors. In *Ginsberg v. New York*, the Court referred to the state's interest in the well-being of its youth as "independent" from its interest in supporting "parents' claim to authority in their own household to direct the rearing of their children."[175] The holding in *Ginsberg*, however, did not turn on whether these interests are independent, and one might argue that they are not because the government's interest in supporting parents lies in assisting them in protecting their children from harmful influences. If "indecent" words are not a harmful influence, then, arguably, the government has no interest, sufficient to override the First Amendment, in supporting parents in their efforts to prevent their children's access to them. A judge has also argued that "a law that effectively *bans* all indecent programming ... does not facilitate parental supervision. In my view, my right as a parent has been preempted, not facilitated, if I am told that certain programming will be banned from my ... television. Congress cannot take away my right to decide what my children watch, absent some showing that my children are in fact at risk of harm from exposure to indecent programming."[176]

If the government could persuade a court that a ban, during certain hours, on the broadcast of "indecent" words regardless of context serves a compelling interest—either in protecting the well-being of minors or in supporting parents' claim to authority—the government would then have to prove that the ban was the least restrictive means to advance that interest. This might raise questions such as whether it is necessary to prohibit particular words on weekdays during school hours, solely to protect pre-school children and children who are home sick some days. In response to this question, the government could note that the broadcast in *Pacifica* was at 2 p.m. on a Tuesday, but was nevertheless considered a "time[ ] of the day when there is a reasonable risk that children may be in the audience."[177] More significantly, however, a court might find a ban too restrictive because it would prohibit the broadcast, between certain hours, of material, including works of art and other material with serious value, that would not attract substantial numbers of youthful viewers or listeners.

In conclusion, it appears that, if a court were to apply strict scrutiny to determine the constitutionality of a ban on the broadcast of "indecent" language regardless of context, then it might require the government to "demonstrate that the recited harms are real, not merely conjectural, and that the regulation will in fact alleviate these harms in a direct and material way." This would mean that the government would have to demonstrate a compelling governmental interest, such as that hearing "indecent" words on broadcast radio and television is harmful to minors, despite the likelihood that minors hear such words elsewhere, or that banning "indecent" words is necessary to support parents' authority in their own household. If the government could not demonstrate a compelling governmental interest, then the court might find the ban unconstitutional. Even if the government could demonstrate a compelling interest, a court might find the ban unconstitutional if it applied to material with serious value, at least if such material would not attract substantial numbers of youthful viewers or listeners.

Whether a court would apply strict scrutiny would depend upon whether, in light of the proliferation of cable television, it finds *Pacifica* to remain applicable to broadcast media. If a court does find that *Pacifica* remains applicable to broadcast media, then the court would be faced with questions that *Pacifica* did not decide: whether, on broadcast radio and television during hours when children are likely to be in the audience, the government may prohibit an "indecent" word used as an occasional expletive, or in material that would not attract substantial numbers of youthful viewers or listeners.

ACKNOWLEDGMENTS

This report was originally written by Henry Cohen, Legislative Attorney.

End Notes

[1] The FCC's indecency regulations only apply to broadcast radio and television, and not to satellite radio or cable television. The distinction between broadcast and cable television arises in part from the fact that the rationale for regulation of broadcast media—the dual problems of spectrum scarcity and signal interference—do not apply in the context of cable. As a result, regulation of cable television is entitled to heightened First Amendment scrutiny. *See Turner Broadcasting v. Federal Communications Commission*, 512 U.S. 622 (1994). Cable television is also distinguished from broadcast television by the fact that cable involves a voluntary act whereby a subscriber affirmatively chooses to bring the material into his or her home. *See Cruz v. Ferre*, 755 F.2d 1415 (11th Cir. 1985).

[2] See CRS Report RL33170, *Constitutionality of Applying the FCC's Indecency Restriction to Cable Television*, by Henry Cohen.

[3] Bono's real name is Paul Hewson.

[4] See *In the Matter of Complaints Against Various Broadcast Licensees Regarding Their Airing of the "Golden Globe Awards" Program*, 18 F.C.C. Rcd. 19859 (2003).

[5] *Id.* at 2.

[6] *Id.*

[7] *Id.* at 3.

[8] *Id.*

[9] "FCC Chairman Seeks Reversal on Profanity," *Washington Post*, January 14, 2004, at E01.

[10] *In the Matter of Complaints Against Various Broadcast Licensees Regarding Their Airing of the "Golden Globe Awards" Program*, File No. EB-03-IH-0110 (March 18, 2004).

[11] http://hraunfoss.fcc.gov/edocs_public/attachmatch/DOC-243435A1.pdf.

[12] *Complaints Against Various Television Licensees Concerning Their February 1, 2004, Broadcast of the Super Bowl XXXVIII Halftime Show*, File No. EB-04-IH-0011 (September 22, 2004) http://www.fcc.gov/eb/Orders/2004/FCC-04-209A1.html.

[13] *Id.*

[14] CBS Corp. v. Federal Communications Commission, 535 F.3d 167 (3d Cir. 2008), *vacated and remanded*, No. 08-653 (U.S. May 4, 2009).

[15] 18 U.S.C. §1464. "Radio communication" includes broadcast television, as the term is defined as "the transmission by radio of writing, signs, signals, pictures, and sounds of all kinds." 47 U.S.C. §153(33).

[16] 47 U.S.C. §503(b).

[17] 438 U.S. 726 (1978).

[18] The United States Court of Appeals for the District of Columbia Circuit had reversed the Commission's order. *See* 556 F.2d 9 (D.C. Cir. 1977). The Commission appealed that decision to the Supreme Court, which reversed the lower court's decision.

[19] 438 U.S. at 732.

[20] *Id.*

[21] *Id.* at 742.

[22] *Id.* at 731; *see, In the Matter of a Citizen's Complaint Against Pacifica Foundation Station WBAI (FM), New York, New York*, 56 F.C.C.2d 94 (1975).

[23] *In the Matter of Pacifica Foundation, Inc. d/b/a Pacifica Radio Los Angeles, California*, 2 F.C.C. Rcd. 2698 (1987). Two other orders handed down the same day articulate the Commission's clarified indecency standard. *See also In the Matter of the Regents of the University of California*, 2 F.C.C. Rcd. 2703 (1987); *In the Matter of Infinity Broadcasting Corporation of Pennsylvania*, 2 F.C.C. Rcd. 2705 (1987).

[24] The Commission noted Arbitron ratings indicating that a number of children remain in the local audience well after 10 p.m. *See* 2 F.C.C. Rcd. 1698, ¶ 16.

[25] 2 F.C.C. Rcd. 2698, 12 and 15.

[26] 852 F.2d 1332, 1344 (1988).

[27] P.L. 100-459, §608.

[28] *Enforcement of Prohibitions Against Broadcast Obscenity and Indecency*, 4 F.C.C. Rcd. 457 (1988).

[29] *Action for Children's Television v. Federal Communications Commission (ACT II)*, 932 F.2d 1504 (1991), *cert. denied*, 503 U.S. 913 (1992).

[30] *Id.* at 1509.

[31] P.L. 102-356, §16, 47 U.S.C. §303 note.

[32] *In the Matter of Enforcement of Prohibitions Against Broadcast Indecency in 18 U.S.C. 1464*, 8 F.C.C. Rcd. 704 (1993).

[33] *Action for Children's Television v. Federal Communications Commission*, 11 F.3d 170 (D.C. Cir. 1993).

[34] 8 F.C.C. Rcd. at 705-706.

[35] 11 F.3d at 171.

[36] *Id.*

[37] *Action for Children's Television v. Federal Communications Commission*, 15 F.3d 186 (D.C. Cir. 1994).

[38] *Action for Children's Television v. Federal Communications Commission (ACT III)*, 58 F.3d 654 (D.C. Cir. 1995), *cert. denied*, 516 U.S. 1043 (1996).

[39] 58 F.3d at 656.

[40] *Enforcement of Prohibitions Against Broadcast Indecency in 18 U.S.C. §1464*, 10 F.C.C. Rcd. 10558 (1995); 47 C.F.R. 73.3999(b). Subsection (b) prohibits the broadcast of material which is obscene without any reference to time of day. Broadcast obscenity will not be discussed in this report. For more information on obscenity, see CRS Report 95-804, *Obscenity and Indecency: Constitutional Principles and Federal Statutes*, by Henry Cohen, and CRS Report 98-670, *Obscenity, Child Pornography, and Indecency: Brief Background and Recent Developments*, by Kathleen Ann Ruane.

[41] 60 FR 44439 (August 28, 1995).

[42] Enforcement actions based on televised broadcast indecency are rare. However, the Commission recently issued a *Notice of Apparent Liability* for the broadcast of indecent material during a televised morning news program. During the program, the show's hosts interviewed performers with a production entitled "Puppetry of the Penis," who appeared wearing capes but were otherwise nude. A performer's penis was exposed during the broadcast. *See In the Matter of Young Broadcasting of San Francisco, Inc.*, File No. EB-02-IH-0786 (January 27, 2004). *See also In the Matter of Complaints Against Various Licensees Regarding Their Broadcast of the Fox Television Network Program "Married by America" on April 7, 2003*, File No. EB-03-IH-0162 (October 12, 2004).

[43] Under 47 U.S.C. §503(b)(2)(A), the maximum fine per violation is $25,000. However, the maximum forfeiture amount was increased to $32,500 pursuant to the Debt Collection Improvement Act of 1996, P.L. 104-134, which amended the Federal Civil Monetary Penalty Inflation Adjustment Act of 1990, P.L. 101-410. *See* 47 C.F.R. §1.80.

[44] Regulations set a maximum forfeiture of $325,000 for any single act or failure to act, which arguably limits the forfeiture for a single broadcast. *See* 47 C.F.R. §1.80.

[45] 47 U.S.C. §503(b)(1)(D) provides that the FCC may impose a forfeiture penalty upon any "person" who violates 18 U.S.C. §1464, which makes it a crime to "utter" indecent language. In addition, 47 U.S.C. §503(b)(6)(B) provides that the FCC may not impose a forfeiture penalty on a person who does not hold a broadcast station license if the violation occurred more than one year prior to the date of issuance of the required notice or notice of apparent liability. This suggests that the FCC may fine a performer if the violation occurred within one year of such date.

[46] *Complaints Against Various Television Licensees Concerning Their February 1, 2004, Broadcast of the Super Bowl XXXVIII Halftime Show*, File No. EB-04-IH-0011 (September 22, 2004) http://www.fcc.gov/eb/Orders/2004/FCC-04-209A1.html.

[47] *See* note 42, *supra*.

[48] *See In the Matter of Industry Guidance on the Commission's Case Law Interpreting 18 U.S.C. §1464 and Enforcement Policies Regarding Broadcast Indecency*, File No. EB-00-IH-0089 (April 6, 2001) http://www.fcc.gov/eb/Orders/2001/fcc01090.html.

[49] *Id.*

[50] *Notice of Apparent Liability, State University of New York*, 8 F.C.C. Rcd. 456 (1993).

[51] *Id.*

[52] *Notice of Apparent Liability, KGB Incorporated*, 7 F.C.C. Rcd. 3207 (1992). *See also Great American Television and Radio Company, Inc.*, 6 F.C.C. Rcd. 3692 (1990); *WIOD, Inc.*, 6 F.C.C. Rcd. 3704 (1989).

[53] 6 F.C.C. Rcd. 3692.

[54] *Notice of Apparent Liability, Citicasters Co.*, 13 F.C.C. Rcd. 22004 (1998).

[55] The Commission has recently indicated that "the mere fact that specific words or phrases are not sustained or repeated does not mandate a finding that material that is otherwise patently offensive to the broadcast medium is not indecent." *In the Matter of Complaints Against Various Broadcast Licensees Regarding the Airing of the "Golden Globe Awards" Program*, File No. EB-03-IH-0110 (March 18, 2004). *See* section entitled "Golden Globe Awards Decision," below.

[56] *L.M. Communications of South Carolina, Inc.*, 7 F.C.C. Rcd. 1595 (1992).

[57] *Id.*

[58] *See Notice of Apparent Liability, Temple Radio, Inc.*, 12 F.C.C. Rcd. 21828 (1997); *Notice of Apparent Liability, EZ New Orleans, Inc.*, 12 F.C.C. Rcd. 4147 (1997).

[59] *Notice of Apparent Liability, Rusk Corporation, Radio Station KLOL*, 5 F.C.C. Rcd. 6332 (1990).

[60] *In the Matter of Application for Review of the Dismissal of an Indecency Complaint Against King Broadcasting Co.*, 5 F.C.C. Rcd. 2971 (1990).

[61] *Id.*

[62] *Id.*

[63] The Commission declined to impose a forfeiture on the broadcast licensees named in the complaint because they were not "on notice" regarding the new interpretations of the Commission's regulations regarding broadcast indecency and the newly adopted definition

of profanity. The Commission also indicated that it will not use its decision in this case adversely against the licensees during the license renewal process.

64 *In the Matter of Complaints Against Various Broadcast Licensees Regarding Their Airing of the "Golden Globe Awards" Program*, File No. EB-03-IH-0110 at 4 (March 18, 2004).

65 *Id.* Similarly, in March, 2006, the FCC decided that "s[***]" has an "inherently excretory connotation" and therefore could not be used from 6 a.m. to 10 p.m. See, *@$#&*% Ken Burns! PBS Scrubbing G.I. Mouths With Soap*, New York Observer, October 2, 2006, p. 1.

66 *Id.* at 5.

67 *Id.* at 6. *See* section entitled "Dwelling or Repetition of Potentially Indecent Material," above.

68 *Id.*

69 *Id.* at 7. Although in this case the Commission found that the broadcast in question was both indecent and profane, there are certain to be words that could be deemed "profane," but do not fit the Commission's definition of "indecent." Under the newly adopted definition of "profanity," many words could arguably be found "profane" because they provoke "violent resentment" or are otherwise "grossly offensive," but not be found "indecent" because they do not refer to any sexual or excretory activity or organ or even "inherently" have a sexual connotation, as the Commission found the phrase that Bono uttered to have. Presumably, it is these words that the Commission will consider on a caseby-case basis.

70 *Id.* at 7, citing Black's Law Dictionary 1210 (6th ed. 1990) and American Heritage College Dictionary 1112 (4th ed. 2002).

71 *Id.*, citing *Tallman v. United States*, 465 F.2d 282, 286 (7th Cir. 1972).

72 *Id.*

73 *Complaints Against Various Television Licensees Concerning Their February 1, 2004, Broadcast of the Super Bowl XXXVIII Halftime Show*, File No. EB-04-IH-0011 (September 22, 2004) http://www.fcc.gov/eb/Orders/2004/FCC-04- 209A1.html.

74 *Id.* at ¶ 11.

75 *Id.* at ¶ 13.

76 *Id.* at ¶ 14.

77 *Id.*

78 *Id.* at ¶¶ 17 - 24.

79 47 C.F.R. §1.80(f)(3).

80 *In the Matter of Complaints Against Various Television Licensees Concerning Their February 1, 2004, Broadcast of the Super Bowl XXXVIII Halftime Show*, File No. EB-04-IH-0011, FCC 06-19 (March 15, 2006).

81 CBS Corp. v. Federal Communications Commission, 535 F.3d 167 (3d Cir. 2008), *vacated and remanded*, No. 08-653 (U.S. May 4, 2009).

82 *In the Matter of Complaints Regarding Various Television Broadcasts Between February 2, 2002 and March 8, 2005*, FCC 06-17 (March 15, 2006).

83 *Id.* Also, three of the programs for which forfeitures were proposed were Spanish-language programs.

84 The Commission found violations, but declined to impose forfeitures with respect to several programs that were aired prior to the Golden Globe Awards Order, at a time when the Commission would not have taken enforcement actions against the isolated use of expletives. *Id.* at 100 - 137.

85 For a complete list of recent actions related to broadcast indecency, see http://transition.fcc.gov/eb/oip/.

86 *In the Matter of Infinity Broadcasting, et al.*, EB-02-IH-0685 (October 2, 2003).

87 *Id.* at 8.

[88] *Id.* at 9. The Commission noted that the contest portion of the broadcast in question lasted over an hour and was reproduced in a 203-page transcript.

[89] *See In the Matter of Viacom Inc., Infinity Radio Inc., et. al.*, FCC 04-268 (November 23, 2004) http://hraunfoss.fcc.gov/edocs_public/attachmatch/FCC-04-268A1.pdf. The decree also covers several other actions pending against Viacom-owned Infinity Radio stations and broadcast television stations, but does not cover the proceedings related to the Super Bowl halftime show discussed *supra.*

[90] *In the Matter of Clear Channel Broadcasting Licenses, Inc., et al.*, File No. EB-02-IH-0261 (January 27, 2004).

[91] *Id.* at 4.

[92] *Id.* at 5.

[93] *Id.* at 6.

[94] *Id.*

[95] *In the Matter of Clear Channel Broadcasting Licensees*, File No. EB-03-IH—159 (April 8, 2004).

[96] *See* Statement of Commissioner Michael J. Copps, http://hraunfoss.fcc.gov/edocs_public /attachmatch/DOC-245911A1.pdf, p. 2.

[97] *See In the Matter of Clear Channel Communications, Inc.*, FCC 04-128 (June 9, 2004) at http://hraunfoss.fcc.gov/edocs_public/attachmatch/FCC-04-128A1.pdf.

[98] *Id.* at 7.

[99] Larry Neumeister, *Appeals court panel grills government lawyer in indecency case*, Associated Press State & Local Wire (December 20, 2006).

[100] Fox Television Stations, Inc. v. Federal Communications Commission, 489 F.3d 444, 447 (2d Cir. 2007), *reversed and remanded*, 129 S. Ct. 1800 (2009).

[101] *Id.*

[102] *Id.* at 462.

[103] Federal Communications Commission v. Fox Television Stations, Inc., 129 S. Ct. 1800 (2009).

[104] *Id.* at 1812.

[105] *Id.* at 1810 (discussing *Motor Vehicle Mfrs. Assn. of United States, Inc. v. State Farm Mut. Autmobile Ins. Co.*, 463 U.S. 29, 43 (1983)). Justice Breyer, in dissent, disagreed with this interpretation of *State Farm*. He argued that, when an agency changes its rules, it must focus on the fact of the change and explaining the change and its basis, which is more than explaining why the new policy is a good one and in keeping with the statute. It includes answering why the change has occurred. In Justice Breyer's opinion, such a requirement does not create a heightened standard, but applies the same standard to different circumstances. According to Justice Breyer, the FCC's failure to adequately explain why it changed policy directions rendered the policy arbitrary and capricious. Id. at 1829.

[106] *Id.* at 1810 (emphasis in original).

[107] *Id.* at 1811.

[108] *Id.* at 1819. In a concurring opinion, Justice Thomas suggested that the viability of the precedents supporting the constitutionality of the FCC's indecency policy may be in doubt. Id. at 1819-22. Justice Thomas therefore appears open to the reconsideration of these precedents.

[109] *Id.* at 462.

[110] *Id.* at 463-465.

[111] Federal Communications Commission v. Fox Television Stations, Inc., 129 S. Ct. 1800, 1819 (2009).

[112] Fox Television Stations, Inc. v. Federal Communications Commission, 613 F. 3d 317 (2d Cir. 2010).

[113] CBS Corp. v. Federal Communications Commission, 535 F.3d 167 (3d Cir. 2008), *vacated and remanded*, No. 08-653 (U.S. May 4, 2009). For a discussion of the incidents giving rise to the FCC's forfeiture order, see the section entitled "Superbowl Half Time Show Decision," *supra*.

[114] *Id.* at 174.

[115] *Id.*

[116] *Id.* at 176-184.

[117] *Id.* at 184.

[118] *Id.* at 184-185.

[119] *Id.* at 188-189.

[120] *Id.* at 189.

[121] *Id.* Upon deciding that the FCC's new policy regarding fleeting images was invalid under the APA, the court was not obligated to reach the second question raised by the case, which was whether CBS had properly been held vicariously liable for the actions of the performers. The court chose, however, to address this question in dicta, and determined that, under two of the FCC's theories of vicarious liability, the fine would have been improperly imposed upon the broadcasters. As to a third FCC theory of vicarious liability, which was that the broadcasters had willfully violated the FCC's regulations by failing to take adequate precautionary measures, the court determined that the definition of "willful" was unclear and remanded the question to the FCC for a decision on that issue. *See* CBS Corp. v. FCC, 535 F.3d 167, 189-209 (3d Cir. 2008).

[122] Petition for Writ of Certiorari, *CBS v. FCC*, No. 08-653.

[123] FCC v. CBS Corp., 129 S. Ct. 2176 (2009).

[124] Fox Television Stations, Inc. v. Federal Communications Commission, 613 F. 3d 317 (2d Cir. 2010).

[125] *Id.* at 327 quoting Farrell v. Burke, 449 F. 3d 470, 485 (2d Cir. 2006)(quoting Grayned v. City of Rockford, 408 U.S. 104, 108 (1972)).

[126] *Id.* at 330.

[127] *Id.* 331.

[128] *Id.*

[129] *Id.*

[130] *Id.* at 332.

[131] *Id.*

[132] *Id.*

[133] *Id.* at 331.

[134] *Id.* at 334.

[135] FCC v. Fox Television, Inc., 2011 U.S. LEXIS 4926 (June 27, 2011).

[136] *FCC v. Fox Television*, 129 S. Ct. at 1820 (Thomas J. concurring).

[137] 438 U.S. 726 (1978). The FCC's action was to issue "a declaratory order granting the complaint," and "state that the order would be 'associated with the station's license file,'" which means that the FCC could consider it when it came time for the station's license renewal. *Id.* at 730.

[138] 521 U.S. 844, 868 (1997) (noting that "the history of the extensive regulation of the broadcast medium" and "the scarcity of available frequencies" are factors "not present in cyberspace," and striking down parts of the Communications Decency Act of 1996). The Court also cited

Pacifica with approval in *United States v. Playboy Entertainment Group, Inc.*, 529 U.S. 803, 813-814 (2000), and in *Ashcroft v. Free Speech Coalition*, 535 U.S. 234, 245 (2002).

[139] Fox Television Stations, Inc. v. Federal Communications Commission, 613 F. 3d at 325 - 327.

[140] *Pacifica*, 438 U.S. at 748,

[141] *Fox Television*, 613 F.3d at 325.

[142] *Id.* at 326.

[143] *Pacifica, supra*, 438 U.S. at 750. A federal court of appeals subsequently held unconstitutional a federal statute that banned "indecent" broadcasts 24 hours a day, but, in a later case, the same court upheld the present statute, 47 U.S.C. §303 note, which bans "indecent" broadcasts from 6 a.m. to 10 p.m. Action for Children's Television v. FCC, 932 F.2d 1504 (D.C. Cir. 1991), *cert. denied*, 503 U.S. 913 (1992); Action for Children's Television v. FCC, 58 F.3d 654 (D.C. Cir. 1995) (en banc), *cert. denied*, 516 U.S. 1043 (1996).

[144] *Id.* at 750, n.29.

[145] *Id.* at 746 n.22. These two sentences and the text accompanying the next footnote, although part of Justice Stevens' opinion, are in a part of the opinion (IV-B) joined by only two other justices. Every other quotation from *Pacifica* in this report was from a part of the opinion that a majority of the justices joined.

[146] *Id.* at 746.

[147] There also appears to be some tension between, on the one hand, Justice Stevens' distinction in *Pacifica* between a point of view and the way in which it is expressed, and, on the other hand, the Court's statement in *Cohen v. California* "that much linguistic expression serves a dual communicative function: it conveys not only ideas capable of relatively precise, detached explication, but otherwise inexpressible emotions as well. In fact, words are often chosen as much for their emotive as their cognitive force. We cannot sanction the view that the Constitution, while solicitous of the cognitive content of individual speech, has little or no regard for that emotive function which, practically speaking, may often be the more important element of the overall message sought to be communicated." 403 U.S. 15, 26 (1971) (upholding the First Amendment right, in the corridor of a courthouse, to wear a jacket bearing the words "F[***] the Draft"). Arguably, Carlin's use of "indecent" words not only served an emotive purpose, but served to indicate the precise words to whose censorship he was objecting. Yet *Pacifica* was decided after *Cohen*, which suggests that *Cohen* does not lessen the precedential value of *Pacifica.*

[148] Miller v. California, 413 U.S. 15, 27, 24 (1973). In addition, in striking down parts of the Communications Decency Act of 1996, the Court expressed concern that the statute may "extend to discussions about prison rape or safe sexual practices, artistic images that include nude subjects, and arguably the card catalogue of the Carnegie Library." *Reno v. ACLU, supra*, 521 U.S. at 878. And, in striking down a federal statute that prohibited child pornography that was produced without the use of an actual child, the Court expressed concern that the statute "prohibits speech despite its serious literary, artistic, political, or scientific value." Ashcroft v. Free Speech Coalition, 535 U.S. 234, 246 (2002). In neither of these cases, however, did the Court state that its holding turned on the statute's application to works of serious value.

[149] 390 U.S. 629 (1968).

[150] *Pacifica, supra*, 438 U.S. at 731-732.

[151] *Id.* at 732 (distinguishing "indecent" from "obscene" and "profane" in 18 U.S.C. §1464).

[152] *Id.* at 740.

[153] *Id.* at 748-750.

[154] 395 U.S. 367, 369 (1969).

[155] *Id.* at 388.

[156] *Id.* at 394.

[157] *Id.* at 396.

[158] 512 U.S. 622, 639 (1994). In *Turner*, the Court held that the "must carry" rules, which "require cable television systems to devote a portion of their channels to the transmission of local broadcast television stations," *id.* at 626, were content-neutral and therefore not subject to strict scrutiny. The Court remanded and ultimately upheld the rules. Turner Broadcasting System, Inc., 520 U.S. 180 (1997).

[159] In the court of appeals decision upholding the current statute that bans "indecent" broadcasts from 6 a.m. to 10 p.m., a dissenting judge wrote of "the utterly irrational distinction that Congress has created between *broadcast* and *cable* operators. No one disputes that cable exhibits more and worse indecency than does broadcast. And cable television is certainly pervasive in our country." Action for Children's Television v. FCC, *supra*, 58 F.3d at 671 (emphasis in original) (Edwards, C.J., dissenting).

[160] 512 U.S. at 638 (citation omitted).

[161] Syracuse Peace Council v. FCC, 867 F.2d 654 (D.C. Cir. 1989), *cert. denied*, 493 U.S. 1019 (1990).

[162] *Id.* at 669. In *Arkansas AFL-CIO v. FCC*, 11 F.3d 1430 (8th Cir. 1993) (en banc), the court of appeals held that Congress had not codified the fairness doctrine and that the FCC's decision to eliminate it was a reasonable interpretation of the statutory requirement that licensees operate in the public interest.

[163] 518 U.S. 727, 748 (1996). The plurality added that cable television "is as 'accessible to children' as over-the-air broadcasting, if not more so," has also "established a uniquely pervasive presence in the lives of all Americans," and can also "'confron[t] the citizen' in 'the privacy of the home,' ... with little or no prior warning." *Id.* at 744-745. Justice Souter concurred that "today's plurality opinion rightly observes that the characteristics of broadcast radio that rendered indecency particularly threatening in *Pacifica*, that is, its intrusion into the house and accessibility to children, are also present in the case of cable television. . . ." *Id.* at 776.

[164] 529 U.S. 803, 813 (2000) (striking down a federal statute that required distributors to fully scramble or fully block signal bleed to non-subscribers to cable channels; "signal bleed" refers to the audio or visual portions of cable television programs that non-subscribers to a cable channel may be able to hear or see despite the fact that the programs have been scrambled to prevent the non-subscribers from hearing or seeing them).

[165] An earlier district court case held that *Pacifica* does not apply to cable television because of several differences between cable and broadcasting. For one, "[i]n the cable medium, the physical scarcity that justifies content regulation in broadcasting is not present." For another, as a subscriber medium, "cable TV is not an intruder but an invitee whose invitation can be carefully circumscribed." Community Television v. Wilkinson, 611 F. Supp. 1099 (D. Utah 1985), *aff'd*, 800 F.2d 989 (10th Cir. 1986), *aff'd*, 480 U.S. 926 (1987) (striking down Utah Cable Television Programming Decency Act). The court of appeals did not discuss the constitutional issue beyond stating that it agreed with the district court's reasons for its holding. 800 F.2d at 991. A summary affirmance by the Supreme Court, as in this case, is "an affirmance of the judgment only," and does not indicate approval of the reasoning of the court below. Mandel v. Bradley, 432 U.S. 173, 176 (1977).

[166] See CRS Report RL33170, *Constitutionality of Applying the FCC's Indecency Restriction to Cable Television*, by Henry Cohen, which concludes that "it appears likely that a court

would find that to apply the FCC's indecency restriction to cable television would be unconstitutional."

[167] *Fox Television*, 613 F.3d at 325-327.

[168] *FCC v. Fox Television*, 129 S. Ct. at1820 (Thomas J. concurring).

[169] Sable Communications of California v. Federal Communications Commission, 492 U.S. 115 (1989); Action for Children's Television v. FCC, *supra*, 932 F.2d at 1509.

[170] *Id.* at 126.

[171] Cohen v. California, *supra*, 403 U.S. at 19, 21. Under *Pacifica*, broadcast media do thrust words upon unwilling or unsuspecting viewers, but, if a court were to apply strict scrutiny to a ban on the broadcast of "indecent" language regardless of context, then it would not be following *Pacifica*.

[172] *Turner Broadcasting, supra*, 512 U.S. at 664 (incidental restriction on speech). *See also*, Edenfield v. Fane, 507 U.S. 761, 770-771 (1993) (restriction on commercial speech); Nixon v. Shrink Missouri Government PAC, 528 U.S. 377, 392 (2000) (restriction on campaign contributions). In all three of these cases, the government had restricted less-thanfully protected speech, so the Court did not apply strict scrutiny. Because offensive words are apparently entitled to full First Amendment protection (except under *Pacifica* and in the instances cited in *Cohen v. California*, quoted in the text above), it seems all the more likely that the Court, if it applied strict scrutiny instead of *Pacifica* to a challenge to a ban on the broadcast of "indecent" words regardless of context, would require the government to demonstrate that harms it recites are real and that the ban would alleviate these harms in a direct and material way.

[173] Interactive Digital Software Association v. St. Louis County, Missouri, 329 F.3d 954, 959 (8th Cir. 2003). The Supreme Court has "recognized that there is a compelling interest in protecting the physical and psychological wellbeing of minors. This interest extends to shielding minors from the influence of literature that is not obscene by adult standards." *Sable, supra*, 492 U.S. at 126. The Court has also upheld a state law banning the distribution to minors of "so-called 'girlie' magazines" even as it acknowledged that "[i]t is very doubtful that this finding [that such magazines are "a basic factor in impairing the ethical and moral development of our youth"] expresses an accepted scientific fact." Ginsberg v. New York, *supra*, 390 U.S. at 631, 641. "To sustain state power to exclude [such material from minors]," the Court wrote, "requires only that we be able to say that it was not irrational for the legislature to find that exposure to material condemned by the statute is harmful to minors." *Id.* at 641. *Ginsberg* thus "invokes the much less exacting 'rational basis' standard of review," rather than strict scrutiny. *Interactive Digital Software Association, supra*, 329 F.3d at 959. A federal district court wrote: "We are troubled by the absence of evidence of harm presented both before Congress and before us that the viewing of signal bleed of sexually explicit programming causes harm to children and that the avoidance of this harm can be recognized as a compelling State interest. We recognize that the Supreme Court's jurisprudence does not require empirical evidence. Only some minimal amount of evidence is required when sexually explicit programming and children are involved." Playboy Entertainment Group, Inc. v. United States, 30 F. Supp.2d 702, 716 (D. Del. 1998), *aff'd*, 529 U.S. 803 (2000). The district court therefore found that the statute served a compelling governmental interest, though it held it unconstitutional because it found that the statute did not constitute the least restrictive means to advance the interest. The Supreme Court affirmed on the same ground, apparently assuming the existence of a compelling governmental interest, but finding a less restrictive means that could have been used.

[174] The full Commission's decision in the Bono case stated that "any use of that word or a variation, in any context, inherently has a sexual connotation." But this does not necessarily mean that it is sexually oriented enough to cause the courts to assume without evidence that it is harmful to minors.

[175] *Ginsberg, supra,* 390 at 640, 639. *See also,* Action for Children's Television v. FCC, *supra,* 58 F.3d at 661.

[176] Action for Children's Television v. FCC, *supra,* 58 F.3d at 670 (emphasis in original) (Edwards, C.J., dissenting).

[177] *Pacifica, supra,* 438 U.S. at 732.

In: Broadcasting, the FCC, Indecency... ISBN: 978-1-62100--775-3
Editors: J. Jefferson and J. McGovern

Chapter 2

CONSTITUTIONALITY OF APPLYING THE FCC'S INDECENCY RESTRICTION TO CABLE TELEVISION*

Henry Cohen

SUMMARY

Various federal officials have spoken in favor of extending the Federal Communication Commission's indecency restriction, which currently applies to broadcast television and radio, to cable and satellite television. This report examines whether such an extension would violate the First Amendment's guarantee of freedom of speech.

The FCC's indecency restriction was enacted pursuant to a federal statute that, insofar as it was found constitutional, requires the FCC to promulgate regulations to prohibit the broadcast of indecent programming from 6 a.m. to 10 p.m. The FCC has found that, for material to be "indecent," it "must describe or depict sexual or excretory organs or activities," and "must be patently offensive as measured by contemporary community standards for the broadcast medium."

In 1978, in Pacifica, the Supreme Court held that, because broadcast radio and television have a "uniquely pervasive presence" and are "uniquely accessible to children," the government may, during certain times of day, prohibit "[p]atently offensive, indecent material" on these

* This is an edited, reformatted and augmented version of a Congressional Research Service publication, CRS Report for Congress, Order Code RL33170, dated March 17, 2008.

media. In 1996, however, a Supreme Court plurality held that, with respect to "how pervasive and intrusive [television] programming is … cable and broadcast television differ little, if at all."

Then, in 2000, the Court held that governmental restrictions on speech on cable television are, unlike those on broadcast media, entitled to strict scrutiny. Thus, whereas, in Pacifica, the Court upheld a restriction on "indecent" material on broadcast media without applying strict scrutiny, the Court apparently would not uphold a comparable restriction on "indecent" material on cable television unless the restriction served a compelling governmental interest by the least restrictive means.

It seems uncertain whether the Court would find that denying minors access to "indecent" material on cable television would constitute a compelling governmental interest. Assuming that it would, then, whether or not there is a less restrictive means than a 6 a.m.-to-10 p.m. ban by which to deny minors access to "indecent" material on cable television, it appears that a strong case may be made that applying the FCC's indecency restrictions to cable television would violate the First Amendment. This is because, as the Supreme Court wrote when it struck down the ban on "indecent" material on the Internet, "the Government may not 'reduc[e] the adult population … to … only what is fit for children.'" In addition, the Court, in the 2000 case mentioned above, struck down a speech restriction on cable television, in part because "for two-thirds of the day no household in those service areas could receive the programming, whether or not the household or the viewer wanted to do so."

Various federal officials have spoken in favor of extending the Federal Communication Commission's indecency restriction,[1] which currently applies to broadcast television and radio, to cable and satellite television.[2] This report examines whether such an extension would violate the First Amendment's guarantee of freedom of speech.

INTRODUCTION

The FCC's indecency restriction was enacted pursuant to a federal statute that, insofar as it was found constitutional, requires the FCC to promulgate regulations to prohibit the broadcast of indecent programming from 6 a.m. to 10 p.m.[3] The FCC has found that, for material to be "indecent," it "must describe or depict sexual or excretory organs or activities," and "must be patently offensive as measured by contemporary community standards for the broadcast medium."[4]

Another federal statute makes it a crime to utter "any obscene, indecent, or profane language by means of radio communication."[5] This statute has been applied to pictures as well as words and to broadcast television as well as radio.[6] In *Federal Communications Commission v. Pacifica Foundation*, the Supreme Court held that the statute does not violate the First Amendment when enforced during hours when children are likely to be in the audience.[7]

The Court in *Pacifica* explained:

> [O]f all forms of communication, it is broadcasting that has received the most limited First Amendment protection. Thus, although other speakers cannot be licensed except under laws that carefully define and narrow official discretion, a broadcaster may be deprived of his license and his forum if the Commission decides that such an action would serve "the public interest, convenience, and necessity." Similarly, although the First Amendment protects newspaper publishers from being required to print the replies of those whom they criticize,
>
> *Miami Herald Publishing Co. v. Tornillo*, 418 U.S. 241, it affords no such protection to broadcasters; on the contrary, they must give free time to the victims of their criticism. *Red Lion Broadcasting Co. v. FCC*, 395 U.S. 367.
>
> The reasons for these distinctions are complex, but two have relevance to the present case. First, the broadcast media have established a uniquely pervasive presence in the lives of all Americans. Patently offensive, indecent material presented over the airwaves confronts the citizen, not only in public, but in the privacy of the home, where the individual's right to be left alone plainly outweighs the First Amendment rights of an intruder. ... To say that one may avoid further offense by turning off the radio when he hears indecent language is like saying that the remedy for an assault is to run away after the first blow.
>
> Second, broadcasting is uniquely accessible to children, even those too young to read. ... Bookstores and motion picture theaters, for example, may be prohibited from making indecent material available to children. We held in *Ginsberg v. New York*, 390 U.S. 629, that the government's interest in the "well-being of its youth" and in supporting "parents' claim to authority in their own household" justified the regulation of otherwise protected expression. ... [8]

In sum, the Court held that, because broadcast radio and television have a "uniquely pervasive presence" and are "uniquely accessible to children," the government may, during certain times of day, prohibit "[p]atently offensive, indecent material" on these media, as such material threatens the well-being of minors and their parents' authority in their own household. Since 1978, however, when the Court decided *Pacifica*, cable television has become more pervasive, thereby rendering broadcast media a less "uniquely pervasive presence." In *Denver Area Educational Telecommunications Consortium, Inc. v. Federal Communications Commission*, a Supreme Court plurality held that, with respect to "how pervasive and intrusive [television] programming is … cable and broadcast television differ little, if at all."[9]

If cable and broadcast television differ little, if at all, then, one might argue, they should be treated alike with regard to indecency restrictions. But does this mean, if one accepts that argument, that cable should be treated like broadcast or that broadcast should be treated like cable? In other words, should cable be made subject to the FCC's indecency restriction, or should broadcast no longer be subject to them? This report will consider these questions from a constitutional standpoint, not from a policy standpoint.

Although one might argue that the fact that broadcast media is no longer uniquely pervasive should render *Pacifica* invalid, no court has found that to be the case, and the Supreme Court has cited *Pacifica* with approval in recent years.[10] The FCC's indecency restriction, therefore, appears to remain constitutional as applied to broadcast media.[11] But would it be constitutional to apply the indecency restriction to cable?

CONSTITUTIONALITY OF APPLYING THE FCC'S INDECENCY RESTRICTION TO CABLE TELEVISION

In *United States v. Playboy Entertainment Group, Inc.*, the Supreme Court held that a content-based speech restriction on cable television "can stand only if it satisfies strict scrutiny. If a statute regulates speech based on its content, it must be narrowly tailored to promote a compelling Government interest. If a less restrictive alternative would serve the Government's purpose, the legislature must use that alternative. To do otherwise would be to restrict speech without an adequate justification, a course the First Amendment does not permit. … It is rare that a regulation restricting speech because of its content will ever be permissible."[12]

The indecency restriction is content-based; therefore, for its application to cable television to be constitutional, it must meet "strict scrutiny," which means that it must promote a compelling governmental interest and be the least restrictive means to do so. This is the same standard that the Supreme Court applies to speech in newspapers, the Internet, and every other medium except broadcast radio and television.[13] The Court does not apply strict scrutiny to broadcast media because, as noted in the above quotation from *Pacifica*, the Court holds that broadcast media have less First Amendment protection than other media.[14] The Court, therefore, did not apply strict scrutiny in *Pacifica*, and the fact that in *Pacifica* it upheld the constitutionality of the indecency restriction as applied to broadcast media does not imply that it would uphold its constitutionality as applied to cable.

Playboy concerned federal restrictions on a type of "indecent" material on cable television: "signal bleed," which refers to images or sounds that come through to non-subscribers, even though cable operators have "used scrambling in the regular course of business, so that only paying customers had access to certain programs."[15] These restrictions, which are found in section 505 of the Communications Decency Act of 1996, require operators of cable channels "primarily dedicated to sexually-oriented programming" to implement more effective scrambling — to fully scramble or otherwise fully block programming so that non-subscribers do not receive it — or to "time channel," which, under an FCC regulation meant to transmit the programming only from 10 p.m. to 6 a.m.[16]

"To comply with the statute," the Court noted, "the majority of cable operators adopted the second, or 'time channeling,' approach. The effect … was to eliminate altogether the transmission of the targeted programming outside the safe harbor period [6 a.m. to 10 p.m.] in affected cable service areas. In other words, for two-thirds of the day no household in those service areas could receive the programming, whether or not the household or the viewer wanted to do so."[17] The Court also noted that "[t]he speech in question was not thought by Congress to be so harmful that all channels were subject to restriction. Instead, the statutory disability applies only to channels 'primarily dedicated to sexually-oriented programming.'"[18]

The Court then applied strict scrutiny to section 505. It did not explicitly say that shielding children from sexually oriented signal bleed was a compelling interest, but it would "not discount the possibility that a graphic image could have a negative impact on a young child."[19] This suggests the possibility that, even if shielding young children from seeing graphic images on cable television is a compelling governmental interest, the Court might not find that shielding older children from such images is a compelling governmental interest. In addition, the Court rejected another interest as compelling: "Even upon the assumption that the Government has an interest in substituting itself for informed and empowered parents, its interest is not sufficiently compelling to justify this widespread restriction on speech."[20] In any case, it was not necessary for the Court to make an explicit finding of a compelling governmental interest, because it held the statute unconstitutional for not constituting the least restrictive means to advance any such interest.

The Court noted that there is "a key difference between cable television and the broadcasting media, which is the point on which this case turns: Cable systems have the capacity to block unwanted channels on a household-by-household basis. ... [T]argeted blocking enables the Government to support parental authority without affecting the First Amendment interests of speakers and willing listeners ...[21] Furthermore, targeted blocking is already required — by section 504 of the Communications Decency Act, which requires cable operators, upon request by a cable service subscriber, to, without charge, fully scramble or otherwise fully block audio and video programming that the subscriber does not wish to receive.[22] "When a plausible, less restrictive alternative is offered to a content-based speech restriction, it is the Government's obligation to prove that the alternative will be ineffective to achieve its goal. The Government has not met that burden here."[23] The Court concluded, therefore, that section 504, with adequate publicity to parents of their rights under it, constituted a less restrictive alternative to section 505.

Applying Strict Scrutiny

We now consider how a court might apply strict scrutiny in determining whether applying the FCC's indecency restriction to cable television would be constitutional. We consider first whether a court would find that applying the restriction to cable television would serve a compelling governmental interest, and then, on the assumption that it would, we consider whether a court would find it the least restrictive means to advance that interest.

Compelling Governmental Interest

When the Court considers the constitutionality of a restriction on speech, it ordinarily — even when the speech that is restricted lacks full First Amendment protection and the Court applies less than strict scrutiny — requires the government to "demonstrate that the recited harms are real, not merely conjectural, and that the regulation will in fact alleviate these harms in a direct and material way."[24] With respect to restrictions designed to deny minors access to sexually explicit material, by contrast, the courts appear to assume, without requiring evidence, that such material is harmful to minors, or to consider it "obscene as to minors," even if it is not obscene as to adults,[25] and therefore not entitled to First Amendment protection with respect to minors, whether it is harmful to them or not.[26] In *Pacifica*, as quoted above, the Court implied that making "indecent" material unavailable to children serves their "well-being."[27]

This is not to say with certainty that the Supreme Court would find a compelling governmental interest in denying minors access to "indecent" material. It might, for example, distinguish among different types of "indecent" material, and, even if it found a compelling governmental interest in denying minors access to sexually explicit material, it might find otherwise with respect to four-letter words, in light of the fact that minors generally hear such words elsewhere than on cable television, and in light of the fact that such words may be used as adjectives or expletives, arguably with no sexual or excretory connotation.[28] The Court might also distinguish among minors of different ages, even with respect to access to sexually explicit material. As noted above, in *Playboy* the Court seemed to leave open the possibility that it might not find a compelling governmental interest in shielding older children from sexually oriented material. In addition, when the Court struck down the portion of the Communications Decency Act of 1996 that prohibited "indecent" material on the Internet, the Court would "neither accept nor reject the Government's submission that the First Amendment does not forbid a blanket prohibition on all 'indecent' and 'patently offensive' messages communicated to a 17-year-old — no matter how much value the message may have and regardless of parental approval. It is at least clear that the strength of the Government's interest in protecting minors is not equally strong throughout the coverage of this broad statute."[29]

The Supreme Court has cited another governmental interest that might be asserted to justify applying the FCC's indecency restriction to cable, but the Court has not stated whether it is "compelling": it is the interest "in supporting 'parents' claim to authority in their own household.'"[30] A dissenting judge has argued that "a law that effectively *bans* all indecent programming … does not facilitate parental supervision. In my view, my right as a parent has been preempted, not facilitated, if I am told that certain programming will be banned from my … television. Congress cannot take away my right to decide what my children watch, absent some showing that my children are in fact at risk of harm from exposure to indecent programming."[31]

Perhaps, however, the Supreme Court would take the approach it did in *Playboy* and focus on the second aspect of strict scrutiny: whether the FCC's indecency restriction is the least restrictive means available to advance the government's interest.

Least Restrictive Means

Assuming for the sake of argument that applying the FCC's indecency restriction to cable television would serve a compelling governmental interest, is there a less restrictive means by which that interest could be served? If so, then applying the FCC's indecency restriction to cable television would be unconstitutional. The Court in *Playboy*, as quoted above, noted that there is "a key difference between cable television and the broadcasting media, which is the point on which this case turns: Cable systems have the capacity to block unwanted channels on a household-by-household basis. ... [T] argeted blocking enables the Government to support parental authority without affecting the First Amendment interests of speakers and willing listeners ... [32]

The targeted blocking, however, that the Court in *Playboy* found to be a less restrictive means to keep signal bleed from viewers who object to it, would not seem as feasible to keep "indecent" material from viewers who object to it. In the case of signal bleed, a viewer could request blocking of channels that he knows to present pornography. By contrast, in order for targeted blocking to keep "indecent" programming from viewers who object to it, viewers would have to know what channels would ever, between 6 a.m. and 10 p.m., allow on any program the utterance of a four-letter word or the exposure of a woman's breast, among other things.[33] For viewers to know this would seem to entail that every channel be required to state whether it will refrain from transmitting "indecent" material on all future programming, and, if a channel stated that it would, to be bound by that statement. This requirement would appear to burden freedom of speech to the extent that it might well violate the First Amendment.[34] It might even be viewed as a prior restraint, and prior restraints are almost always unconstitutional.[35]

To the extent that technology allows viewers to block particular programs as opposed to entire channels, the same First Amendment difficulties would apparently arise. For such blocking to be effective, producers who did not wish to be blocked for transmitting "indecent" programming would have to agree to refrain from ever allowing the utterance of a four-letter word on a program, even if the program ordinarily contained nothing deemed "indecent."

Thus, there may be no less restrictive means that would be constitutional to keep "indecent" material off cable television during certain hours than to apply the FCC's indecency restrictions.[36] This, however, would not necessarily mean that to apply them to cable television would be constitutional. Two federal courts of appeals have written that "[t]he State may not regulate at all if it turns out that even the least restrictive means of regulation is still unreasonable when its limitations on freedom of speech are balanced against the benefits gained from those limitations."[37] The more recent of these cases affirmed a preliminary injunction against the enforcement of the Child Online Protection Act, which banned material that is "harmful to minors" from the Internet.[38] The older case upheld FCC regulations that implemented a statute that restricted minors' access to obscene "dial-a-porn" services.

It appears that a strong case may be made that applying the FCC's indecency restriction to cable television would be "unreasonable" under the above court of appeals' formulation. This is because, as the Supreme Court wrote when it struck down the ban on "indecent" material on the Internet, "the Government may not 'reduc[e] the adult population … to … only what is fit for children.' '[R]egardless of the strength of the government's interest' in protecting children, '[t]he level of discourse reaching a mailbox simply cannot be limited to that which would be suitable for a sandbox.'"[39]

One might reply that to apply the FCC's indecency restriction to cable would limit the adult population's discourse only from 6 a.m. to 10 p.m. But the fact the Supreme Court in *Pacifica* upheld such a limitation on broadcast media does not mean that it would uphold it on cable television. In *Pacifica*, as noted, the Court did not apply strict scrutiny. In *Playboy*, where the Court did apply strict scrutiny to a speech restriction on cable television, it held the speech restriction unconstitutional, in part because, as quoted above, "for two-thirds of the day no household in those service areas could receive the programming, whether or not the household or the viewer wanted to do so."[40] In addition, the Court struck down the ban in the Communications Decency Act of 1996 on "indecent" material on the Internet, notwithstanding that such material is available to adults in other media.[41] It seems clear that governmental restrictions of fully protected speech, including "indecent" material on cable television, are unconstitutional unless they pass strict scrutiny, even if they do not close all outlets for such speech.

SUMMARY AND CONCLUSION

In 1978, in *Pacifica*, the Supreme Court held that, because broadcast radio and television have a "uniquely pervasive presence" and are "uniquely accessible to children," the government may, during certain times of day, prohibit "[p]atently offensive, indecent material" on these media. In 1996, however, in *Denver Area Consortium,* a Supreme Court plurality held that, with respect to "how pervasive and intrusive [television] programming is … cable and broadcast television differ little, if at all."

The fact that a plurality of the Court views cable and broadcast television as differing little with respect to their pervasiveness and intrusiveness might suggest that the Court would apply the First Amendment to both media in the same way. The Court, however, continues to cite *Pacifica* with approval, but, in *Playboy*, it held that governmental restrictions on cable television are, unlike those on broadcast media, entitled to strict scrutiny. Thus, whereas, in *Pacifica*, the Court upheld a restriction on "indecent" material on broadcast media without applying strict scrutiny, the Court apparently would not uphold a comparable restriction on "indecent" material on cable television unless the restriction served a compelling governmental interest by the least restrictive means.

It seems uncertain whether the Court would find that denying minors access to "indecent" material on cable television would constitute a compelling governmental interest. Although the Court has held that denying minors access to sexually explicit material constitutes a compelling governmental interest, not all "indecent" material is sexually explicit. In addition, the Court has suggested that it may not view minors of all ages identically for First Amendment purposes.

Assuming for the sake of argument that the Court would find a compelling governmental interest in denying minors access to "indecent" material on cable television, there does not appear to be a less restrictive means than the FCC's restrictions to advance this interest, other than banning "indecent" material for fewer hours per day. The lack of a less restrictive means, however, would not necessarily mean that to apply the FCC's restrictions to cable television would be constitutional. This is because, as two federal courts of appeals have written, "[t]he State may not regulate at all if it turns out that even the least restrictive means of regulation is still unreasonable when its limitations on freedom of speech are balanced against the benefits gained from those limitations." The Supreme Court has not spoken on this proposition, however.

It appears that a strong case may be made that applying the FCC's indecency restriction to cable television would be "unreasonable" under this formulation. This is because, as the Supreme Court wrote when it struck down the ban on "indecent" material in the Internet, "the Government may not 'reduc[e] the adult population ... to ... only what is fit for children.'" In *Playboy*, the Court, applying strict scrutiny, struck down a speech restriction on cable television, in part because "for two-thirds of the day no household in those service areas could receive the programming, whether or not the household or the viewer wanted to do so." Thus, it appears likely that a court would find that to apply the FCC's indecency restriction to cable television would be unconstitutional.

End Notes

[1] 47 C.F.R. § 73.3999(b).

[2] This report hereinafter does not refer to satellite television, but its references to cable television to may read to include satellite television. For references to support for applying the indecency restriction to cable television, see, e.g., Paul K. McMasters, *Inside the First Amendment: Surrendering our choices to a sense of decency*, Gannet News Service (April 11, 2005); Drew Clark, *Lawmakers May Only Be Partially Pleased by Cable*, National Journal's Technology Daily (April 4, 2005).

[3] 47 U.S.C. § 303 note; Action for Children's Television v. Federal Communications Commission, 58 F.3d 654 (D.C. Cir. 1995) (en banc), *cert. denied*, 516 U.S. 1043 (1996) (striking down the statute insofar as it banned "indecent programming" on non-public broadcast stations from 10 p.m. to midnight).

[4] *In the Matter of Industry Guidance on the Commission's Case Law Interpreting 18 U.S.C. § 1464 and Enforcement Policies Regarding Broadcast Indecency*, File No. EB-00-IH-0089 (April 6, 2001). [http://www.fcc.gov/eb/Orders/2001/fcc01090.html].

[5] 18 U.S.C. § 1464.

[6] *See*, e.g., *Complaints Against Various Television Licensees Concerning Their February 1, 2004, Broadcast of the Super Bowl XXXVIII Halftime Show*, File No. EB-04-IH-0011 (September 22, 2004).

[7] 438 U.S. 726 (1978) ("It is appropriate, in conclusion, to emphasize the narrowness of our holding. . . . The time of day was emphasized by the Commission. The content of the program in which the language is used will also affect the composition of the audience." *Id.* at 750). A federal court of appeals later declared a 24-hour-a-day ban unconstitutional. *Action for Children's Television v. Federal Communications Commission*, 932 F.2d 1504 (D.C. Cir. 1991), *cert denied*, 503 U.S. 913 (1992).

[8] *Id.* at 748-749.

[9] 518 U.S. 727, 748 (1996). The plurality, quoting words from *Pacifica* that appear in the indented quotation above, added that cable television "is as 'accessible to children' as overthe-air broadcasting, if not more so," has also "established a uniquely pervasive presence in the lives of all Americans," and can also "'confron[t] the citizen' in 'the privacy

of the home,' . . . with little or no prior warning." *Id.* at 744-745. Justice Souter concurred that "today's plurality opinion rightly observes that the characteristics of broadcast radio thatrendered indecency particularly threatening in *Pacifica*, that is, its intrusion into the house and accessibility to children, are also present in the case of cable television. . . ." *Id.* at 776.

[10] Reno v. American Civil Liberties Union, 521 U.S. 844, 868 (1997); United States v. Playboy Entertainment Group, Inc., 529 U.S. 803, 813 (2000); Ashcroft v. Free Speech Coalition, 535 U.S. 234, 245 (2002).

[11] This is not to say that every application of them by the FCC is necessarily constitutional. The FCC's application of the restrictions to Bono's single use of a four-letter word as a modifier, and to Janet Jackson's "wardrobe malfunction" during a Superbowl halftime show, are being challenged; *see* CRS Report RL32222, *Regulation of Broadcast Indecency: Background and Legal Analysis*, by Henry Cohen and Kathleen Ann Ruane.

[12] *Playboy, supra* note 10, at 813, 818 (citations omitted).

[13] The Court in *Playboy* wrote, however, "Cable television, like broadcast media, presents unique problems, which inform our assessment of the interests at stake, and which may justify restrictions that would be unacceptable in other contexts." *Id.* Nevertheless, because the Court applied strict scrutiny in *Playboy*, this comment apparently means not that the Court would apply less than strict scrutiny to restrictions on cable television, but that applying strict scrutiny to restrictions on cable television might involve considerations not present when applying it to restrictions on other media.

[14] The lower level of First Amendment protection for broadcast media dates back to *Red Lion Broadcasting Co. v. Federal Communications Commission*, 395 U.S. 367, 369 (1969), in which the Supreme Court upheld the FCC's "fairness doctrine," which "imposed on radio and television broadcasters the requirement that discussion of public issues be presented on broadcast stations, and that each side of those issues must be given fair coverage." The reason that the Court upheld the imposition of the fairness doctrine on broadcast media, though it would not uphold its imposition on print media, is that "[w]here there are substantially more individuals who want to broadcast than there are frequencies to allocate, it is idle to posit an unabridgeable First Amendment right to broadcast comparable to the right of every individual to speak, write, or publish." *Id.* at 388. In *Turner Broadcasting System, Inc. v. Federal Communications Commission*, 512 U.S. 622, 639 (1994), the Court held that this "spectrum scarcity" problem does not apply to cable television. In *Denver Area, supra* note 9, 518 U.S. at 748, the Court noted that spectrum scarcity, in any event, "has little to do with a case that involves the effects of television viewing on children. Those effects are the result of . . . how pervasive and intrusive that programming is."

[15] *Id.* at 806.

[16] 47 U.S.C. § 561.

[17] *Playboy, supra* note 10, at 806-807.

[18] *Id.* at 812.

[19] *Id.* at 826.

[20] *Id.* at 825.

[21] *Id.* at 815.

[22] 47 U.S.C. § 560.

[23] *Playboy, supra* note 10, 529 U.S. at 816.

[24] *Turner Broadcasting, supra* note 14, 512 U.S. at 664 (incidental restriction on speech). *See also*, Edenfield v. Fane, 507 U.S. 761, 770-771 (1993) (restriction on commercial speech); Nixon v. Shrink Missouri Government PAC, 528 U.S. 377, 392 (2000) (restriction on

campaign contributions). In all three of these cases, the government had restricted lessthan-fully protected speech, so the Court did not apply strict scrutiny. Because "indecent" material is generally entitled to full First Amendment protection (except on broadcast media), one might expect that the Court, in determining the constitutionality of applying the FCC's indecency restriction to cable television, would be all the more likely to require the government to demonstrate that harms it recites are real and that the indecency restriction would alleviate these harms in a direct and material way. But see the next sentence in the text.

[25] Material that is obscene as to adults is not entitled to First Amendment protection, whether or not it is harmful to adults. *Miller v. California*, 413 U.S. 15 (1973); *see* CRS Report 95-804, *Obscenity and Indecency: Constitutional Principles and Federal Statutes*, by Henry Cohen.

[26] Interactive Digital Software Association v. St. Louis County, Missouri, 329 F.3d 954, 959 (8th Cir. 2003). The Supreme Court has "recognized that there is a compelling interest in protecting the physical and psychological well-being of minors. This interest extends to shielding minors from the influence of literature that is not obscene by adult standards." *Sable Communications of California v. Federal Communications Commission*, 492 U.S. 115, 126 (1989). The Court has also upheld a state law banning the distribution to minors of "so-called 'girlie' magazines," even as it acknowledged that "[i]t is very doubtful that this finding [that such magazines are "a basic factor in impairing the ethical and moral development of our youth"] expresses an accepted scientific fact." *Ginsberg v. New York*, 390 U.S. 629, 631, 641. "To sustain state power to exclude [such material from minors]," the Court wrote, "requires only that we be able to say that it was not irrational for the legislature to find that exposure to material condemned by the statute is harmful to minors." *Id.* at 641. *Ginsberg* thus "invokes the much less exacting 'rational basis' standard of review," rather than strict scrutiny. *Interactive Digital Software Association*, *supra*, 329 F.3d at 959.

In addition, before *Playboy* reached the Supreme Court, a federal district court wrote:

> We are troubled by the absence of evidence of harm presented both before Congress and before us that the viewing of signal bleed of sexually explicit programming causes harm to children and that the avoidance of this harm can be recognized as a compelling State interest. We recognize that the Supreme Court's jurisprudence does not require empirical evidence. Only some minimal amount of evidence is required when sexually explicit programming and children are involved.

Playboy Entertainment Group, Inc. v. United States, 30 F. Supp.2d 702, 716 (D. Del. 1998), *aff'd*, 529 U.S. 803 (2000). The district court therefore found that the statute served a compelling governmental interest, though it held it unconstitutional because it found that the statute did not constitute the least restrictive means to advance the interest. As noted in the text above, the Supreme Court affirmed on the same ground.

In another case, a federal court of appeals, upholding the FCC's indecency restrictions as applied to broadcast media, noted "that the Supreme Court has recognized that the Government's interest in protecting children extends beyond shielding them from physical and psychological harm. The statute that the Court found constitutional in *Ginsberg* sought to protect children from exposure to materials that would 'impair[ ] [their] *ethical and moral*development. . . . Congress does not need the testimony of psychiatrists and social scientists in order to take note of the coarsening of impressionable minds that can result from a persistent exposure to sexually explicit material. . . .'" *Action for Children's*

Television v. Federal Communications Commission, supra note 3, 58 F.3d at 662 (brackets and italics supplied by the court of appeals). A dissenting judge in the case noted that, "[t]here is not one iota of evidence in the record . . . to support the claim that exposure to indecency is harmful — indeed, the nature of the alleged 'harm' is never explained." *Id.* at 671 (Edwards, C.J., dissenting).

[27] *See*, note 8, *supra*.

[28] The FCC ruled that "given the core meaning of the 'F-Word,' any use of that word, or a variation, in any context, inherently has a sexual connotation. . . ." In the Matter of Complaints Against Various Broadcast Licensees Regarding Their Airing of the "Golden Globe Awards" Program, File No. EB-03-IH-0110 (March 18, 2004). The U.S. Court of Appeals for the Second Circuit, however, found that this view "defies any commonsense understanding of these words, which, as the general public knows, are often used in everyday conversation without any 'sexual or excretory' meaning." Fox Television Stations, Inc. v. Federal Communications Commission, 489 F.3d 444, 459 (2d Cir. 2007), *cert. granted*, No. 07-582 (U.S. March 17, 2008).

[29] Reno v. American Civil Liberties Union, *supra* note 10, 521 U.S. at 878.

[30] *Pacifica, supra* note 7, 438 U.S. at 749, quoting *Ginsberg, supra* note 26, 390 U.S. at 639. *See also, Playboy, supra* note 10, 529 U.S. at 815.

[31] Action for Children's Television v. Federal Communications Commission, *supra* note 3, 58 F.3d at 670 (emphasis in original) (Edwards, C.J., dissenting).

[32] *Playboy, supra* note 10, 529 U.S. at 815.

[33] One commentator, referring to the present CRS report, writes, "The Congressional Research Service misses an important distinction. In *Playboy*, the Court was dealing with a new federal statute that would lead to a 6:00 - 10:00 p.m. ban on indecent material being aired on *primarily sexually-explicit channels*. By its very definition, this was *expected* indecency, and the lockbox and other technological solutions . . . would actually work as intended. . . . For a pay-per-view cable channel that peddles exclusively in smut, blocking technologies are highly effective remedies. The problem is that blocks are totally ineffective when dealing with *unexpected* indecency. Protecting the children, while not compelling enough to warrant a draconian block on all sexual programming from adults who explicitly request it, is likely still compelling enough to warrant the prohibition of indecency on general cable channels." Matthew S. Schwartz, *A Decent Proposal: The Constitutionality of Indecency Regulation on Cable and Direct Broadcast Satellite Services*, 13 Richmond Journal of Law and Technology 17, 27 (2007). In fact, the sentence of the text above that ends with the present footnote — and the sentence has not been revised since the first edition of this report — makes the distinction to which the commentator refers. This report, however, explains below why this distinction may be insufficient to make the extension of the FCC's indecency rule to cable television constitutional.

[34] "The distinction between laws burdening and laws banning speech is but a matter of degree. The Government's content-based burdens must satisfy the same rigorous scrutiny as it content-based bans." *Playboy, supra* note 10, at 812.

[35] *See* CRS Report 95-815, *Freedom of Speech and Press: Exceptions to the First Amendment,* by Henry Cohen.

[36] The government could, of course, reduce the numbers of hours per day that it bans "indecent" material, though the Supreme Court might be less likely to find a compelling governmental interest in a shorter ban, because a shorter ban would be less effective in denying minors access to "indecent" material.

[37] American Civil Liberties Union v. Reno, 217 F.3d 162, 179 (3d Cir. 2000), *vacated and remanded on other grounds sub nom.*, Ashcroft v. American Civil Liberties Union, 535 U.S. 564 (2002), quoting Carlin Communications, Inc. v. Federal Communications Commission, 837 F.2d 546, 555 (2d Cir. 1988), *cert. denied*, 488 U.S. 924 (1988).

[38] In *Reno v. American Civil Liberties Union, supra* note 10, 521 U.S. 844 (1997), the Supreme Court struck down the Communications Decency Act of 1996, which banned "indecent" material on the Internet, and, in *Ashcroft v. American Civil Liberties Union*, 542 U.S. 656 (2004) (a second Supreme Court decision in *American Civil Liberties Union v. Reno*, *supra* note 37), the Court upheld a preliminary injunction against enforcement of the Child Online Protection Act, which banned "harmful to minors" material on the Internet. In both cases, the Court applied strict scrutiny and suggested that filtering software might be a less restrictive alternative. 521 U.S. at 844; 542 U.S. at 668. This alternative, of course, would not be an option with respect to cable television.

[39] *Reno*, *supra* note 10, 521 U.S. at 875 (citations omitted).

[40] *Playboy*, *supra* note 10, at 806-807.

[41] *Reno*, *supra* note 10.

In: Broadcasting, the FCC, Indecency...
Editors: J. Jefferson and J. McGovern
ISBN: 978-1-62100--775-3

Chapter 3

FAIRNESS DOCTRINE: HISTORY AND CONSTITUTIONAL ISSUES*

Kathleen Ann Ruane

SUMMARY

The Fairness Doctrine was a policy of the Federal Communications Commission (FCC or Commission) that required broadcast licensees to cover issues of public importance and to do so in a fair manner. Issues of public importance were not limited to political campaigns. Nuclear plant construction, workers' rights, and other issues of focus for a particular community could gain the status of an issue that broadcasters were required to cover. Therefore, the Fairness Doctrine was distinct from the so-called "equal time" rule, which requires broadcasters to grant equal time to qualified candidates for public office, because the Fairness Doctrine applied to a much broader range of topics.

In 1987, after a period of study, the FCC repealed the Fairness Doctrine. The FCC found that the doctrine likely violated the free speech rights of broadcasters, led to less speech about issues of public importance over broadcast airwaves, and was no longer required because of the increase in competition among mass media. The repeal of the doctrine did not end the debate among lawmakers, scholars, and others about its constitutionality and impact on the availability of diverse information to the public.

* This is an edited, reformatted and augmented version of a Congressional Research Service publication, CRS Report for Congress R40009, from www.crs.gov, dated July 13, 2011.

The debate in Congress regarding whether to reinstate the doctrine continues today. Recently, Chairman Upton of the House Subcommittee on Communications and Technology sent a letter to FCC Chairman Genachowski urging the Commission to remove the regulations relating to the Fairness Doctrine from the Code of Federal Regulations. Chairman Genachowski responded by reasserting his lack of support for the Fairness Doctrine and agreeing to begin the process of repealing the regulations.

Any attempt to reinstate the Fairness Doctrine likely would be met with a constitutional challenge. Those opposing the doctrine would argue that it violates their First Amendment rights. In 1969, the Supreme Court upheld the constitutionality of the Fairness Doctrine, but applied a lower standard of scrutiny to the First Amendment rights of broadcasters than it applies to other media. Since that decision, the Supreme Court's reasoning for applying a lower constitutional standard to broadcasters' speech has been questioned. Furthermore, when repealing the doctrine, the FCC found that, as the law stood in 1987, the Fairness Doctrine violated the First Amendment even when applying the lower standard of scrutiny to the doctrine. No reviewing court has examined the validity of the agency's findings on the constitutional issue. Therefore, whether a newly instituted Fairness Doctrine would survive constitutional scrutiny remains an open question.

INTRODUCTION

For over 30 years, the Federal Communications Commission (FCC or Commission) required broadcast licensees to present controversial issues of public importance and to do so in a manner that was fair and balanced. This requirement came to be known as the "Fairness Doctrine." In practice, it required broadcasters to identify issues of public importance, decide to cover those issues, and then to afford the best representatives of the opposing views on the issue the opportunity to present their case to the community.

Many broadcasters complained that the Fairness Doctrine was overly burdensome and inhibited their ability to cover issues of public importance. Those in favor of the doctrine believed that it ensured vibrant discussion over the public airwaves. After a number of proceedings examining the effects of the Fairness Doctrine on broadcasters, the FCC abolished the doctrine in 1987. The FCC reasoned that increased competition in the marketplace, First Amendment concerns, and evidence that the Fairness Doctrine actually chilled speech rather than facilitating it justified abandoning the policy.

Discussion continues among scholars and lawmakers regarding the Fairness Doctrine's effectiveness, constitutionality, and reinstatement. Some believe the Fairness Doctrine should be resurrected to promote public discourse, while others believe the doctrine should never be reinstated because it inhibits the free exchange of ideas. For example, as recently as the 109th Congress, bills were introduced in Congress to reinstate the Fairness Doctrine. On the other hand, in the 111th Congress, there have been a number of bills introduced that would prevent the FCC from reinstating the Fairness Doctrine.

This report will discuss the history of the Fairness Doctrine, enforcement of the doctrine by the FCC, abolition of it by the FCC, efforts to effect and to prevent its reinstatement, and potential constitutional issues with reinstating the doctrine as applied to broadcasters and as applied to satellite and cable television providers. It will be updated as warranted.

THE FAIRNESS DOCTRINE

Foundations of the Fairness Doctrine

Early communications legislation established the American system for broadcasting, in which licenses to broadcast are granted to private individuals (or corporations).[1] Those without a license are not permitted to broadcast.[2] This scheme prevents interference from competing broadcasters. It also guarantees that some speakers who wish to communicate via broadcast airwaves cannot do so.

Recognizing that this structure prevented many who would wish to communicate via broadcast from doing so, and that individuals who were able to obtain a license had control over the content the stations broadcast, Congress required that broadcast licenses may be granted only when the licenses serve the public interest.[3] The FCC is charged with enforcing this provision by considering the public interest when granting licenses to broadcasters, renewing them, and modifying them.[4] Furthermore, the FCC is required "from time to time, as public convenience, interest or necessity requires" to promulgate "such rules and regulations and prescribe such restrictions and conditions ... as may be necessary to carry out the provisions of" the Communications Act.[5] The Supreme Court has noted that these provisions provide the FCC with an expansive mandate to ensure that broadcast stations operate in the public interest.[6]

In the spirit of this broad mandate, the FCC favored granting and renewing licenses to broadcast stations that presented more than one viewpoint in their programming. This preference evolved over time. In 1949, finding its authority in the public interest obligations imposed upon broadcasters by the Communications Act, the FCC issued a report entitled *In the Matter of Editorializing by Broadcast Licensees*.[7] The report affirmatively established the duty of broadcast licensees to cover controversial issues of public importance in a fair and balanced manner. The obligation is known as the Fairness Doctrine.[8]

The Fairness Doctrine consisted of two basic requirements:

1. that every licensee devote a reasonable portion of broadcast time to the discussion and consideration of controversial issues of public importance; and
2. that in doing so, [the broadcaster must be] fair – that is, [the broadcaster] must affirmatively endeavor to make ... facilities available for the expression of contrasting viewpoints held by responsible elements with respect to the controversial issues presented.[9]

These obligations were not satisfied by simply granting air time to those who requested it in order to respond to an issue previously discussed during the broadcaster's regular programming.[10] Broadcasters instead had the affirmative duty to determine what the appropriate opposing viewpoints were on these controversial issues, and who was best suited to present them.[11] If sponsored programming was not an option, the broadcasters had to provide it at their own expense.[12]

Further requirements of the Fairness Doctrine were eventually codified into regulation. The personal attack rule stated that when personal attacks were made on individuals involved in public issues, the broadcaster had to, within one week of the broadcast, notify the person attacked, provide him with a copy of the broadcast (either script or tape), and allow him an opportunity to respond over the broadcaster's facilities.[13] The political editorial rule required that when a broadcaster endorsed a particular political candidate, the broadcaster was required to provide the other qualified candidates for the same office (or their representatives) the opportunity to respond over the broadcaster's facilities.[14]

Congress amended Section 315 of the Communications Act in 1959 to include what seemed to be a tacit approval of the FCC's Fairness Doctrine.[15] Section 315 imposes the requirement upon broadcasters to grant equal broadcasting time to political candidates with certain exceptions. The amendment pertaining to the Fairness Doctrine states the following:

> Nothing in the foregoing sentence [creating exemptions from the equal time requirements] shall be construed as relieving broadcasters, in connection with the presentation of newscasts, news interviews, news documentaries, and on-the-spot, from the obligation imposed upon them under this chapter to operate in the public interest and to afford reasonable opportunity for the discussion of conflicting views on issues of public importance.

In its report on the amendment, the House explained that this provision "is a restatement of the basic policy of the 'standard of fairness' which is imposed on broadcasters under the Communications Act of 1934."[16] Debate arose in subsequent years over whether this addition to Section 315 codified the Fairness Doctrine, or merely stated Congress's intent to avoid interference with the FCC's enforcement of the Fairness Doctrine. This debate will be addressed in full in the section of this report addressing the repeal of the Fairness Doctrine.

Enforcement of the Fairness Doctrine

In reviewing particular broadcasts for potential violations of the Fairness Doctrine, the FCC looked to whether the licensee had acted "reasonably and in good faith to present a fair cross-section of opinion on the controversial issue."[17] The FCC emphasized that harmless errors and honest mistakes were not actionable and that the merits of the actual competing viewpoints presented were not under review by the agency. By way of example, in the course of enforcing the doctrine, the FCC found that the establishment of a National Fair Employment Practices Commission was an issue of public importance that triggered Fairness Doctrine obligations, as were issues such as the potential institution of pay TV, a nutritionist giving advice about diet and health, programs describing socialist forms of government, etc.[18] Consequences for failure to comply with the Fairness Doctrine could have ranged anywhere from a requirement that time be granted to unaired viewpoints, to punishment as severe as a loss of license or a substantial demerit in a comparative renewal proceeding.[19]

Red Lion Broadcasting Co., Inc. v. FCC

In *Red Lion Broadcasting Co., Inc. v. Federal Communications Commission* (*Red Lion*), decided in 1969, the Supreme Court took up two questions related to the Fairness Doctrine. First, the Court addressed whether the FCC had the authority to create and to enforce the Fairness Doctrine.[20] Second, the Court examined whether requiring broadcasters to cover issues of public importance and to present opposing views on those issues fairly violated the broadcasters' First Amendment rights to free speech.

Specifically at issue in *Red Lion* were the personal attack and political editorial rules noted above. Two separate cases had been consolidated for review by the Supreme Court. In the first case, the Red Lion Broadcasting Company (a Pennsylvania radio station) had broadcast a program in which Reverend Billy James Hargis described author Fred J. Cook as having been fired for making false charges against city officials, having worked for a Communist-affiliated publication, having defended Alger Hiss, and having attacked J. Edgar Hoover.[21] Cook heard the broadcast and demanded reply time, but the station refused. The FCC found that the station had failed to meet its obligations under the Fairness Doctrine, a decision that was upheld on appeal to the Court of Appeals for the D.C. Circuit. The broadcast station appealed to the Supreme Court. The second case was a direct challenge to the constitutionality of the political editorial and personal attack regulation. The regulations were held to be unconstitutional under the First Amendment by the Seventh Circuit Court of Appeals and the FCC appealed.

The Supreme Court found that the FCC was within its authority to implement the regulations at issue in the second case and to issue the decision in *Red Lion.*[22] In the estimation of the Court, the agency was implementing the policy of Congress "rather than embarking on a frolic of its own." The Court traced the history of the Fairness Doctrine, noting that broadcast spectrum was originally unregulated and the result was chaos. The Court found that Congress decided that the best solution was to take control of access to the broadcast spectrum and regulate its allocation in a manner consistent with the public interest. Congress granted the power to choose broadcast licensees to the FCC and instructed the agency to consider the public interest when exercising that power.

In order to exercise that authority, the Supreme Court noted that the FCC needed to determine what broadcasting in the public interest meant. From its inception, the FCC (and its predecessor agency, the Federal Radio Commission) held the view that the "public interest requires ample play for the free and fair competition of opposing views, and the Commission believes that the principle applies ... to all discussion of issues of importance to the public."[23] Enforcement of this general policy continued until the FCC issued its report *In the Matter of Editorializing by Broadcast Licensees* in 1949, which set out the basic requirements of the Fairness Doctrine as it would exist throughout its life.[24] Then in 1959, Congress chose to include in its amendment to Section 315 of the Communications Act of 1934 a specific ratification of the Fairness Doctrine. In light of this evidence, the Supreme Court held that the Fairness Doctrine was a legitimate exercise of the FCC's congressionally delegated authority.

The broadcasters also argued that the Fairness Doctrine impinged upon their First Amendment right to freedom of speech. They contended that it was their right to broadcast whatever they chose and to exclude whom they wished from their frequencies. The Supreme Court rejected this argument for a number of reasons, but the most often cited has come to be known as the scarcity rationale. The Court said:

> Because of the scarcity of radio frequencies, the Government is permitted to put restraints on licensees in favor of others whose views should be expressed on this unique medium. But the people as a whole retain their interest in free speech by radio and their collective right to have the medium function consistently with the ends and purposes of the First Amendment. It is the right of the viewers and listeners, not the right of the broadcasters, which is paramount.[25]

The Supreme Court, therefore, upheld the constitutionality of the Fairness Doctrine and the personal attack/political editorial regulation. However, the history of the doctrine would not end there.

Repeal by the FCC

In the 1980s, the FCC began to question the continued necessity of the Fairness Doctrine. As a result, the Commission undertook to examine its application of the Fairness Doctrine, the doctrine's effects on broadcasters, and the constitutionality of the doctrine in light of developments in First Amendment law.[26] In 1985, the FCC released an order addressing three main questions related to the Fairness Doctrine: (1) whether the doctrine was constitutionally permissible under then-current marketplace conditions and

First Amendment Jurisprudence; (2) whether the doctrine actually chilled rather than encouraged free speech; and, (3) whether the doctrine was codified into law by either Section 315 or the general public interest standard in the Communications Act.[27]

The Commission acknowledged that the Supreme Court had upheld the constitutionality of the Fairness Doctrine in *Red Lion*, but determined nonetheless that the constitutionality of the Fairness Doctrine had become suspect.[28] The Commission looked to the development of First Amendment law following the *Red Lion* decision and determined that the evolution of free speech in mass communications cases along with developments in broadcast technology potentially undermined the constitutionality of the Fairness Doctrine.[29] The FCC recognized, however, that it is the province of the courts to pass upon the constitutionality of its policies and declined to pass on the constitutionality of the doctrine.

The Commission examined the effect of its enforcement of the Fairness Doctrine upon broadcasters and came to the conclusion that the doctrine chilled speech substantially.[30] The Commission noted that enforcement actions usually occurred under the second prong of the Fairness Doctrine. In other words, broadcasters most often were determined to have violated the doctrine by failing to provide all valid opposing viewpoints air time on a given issue. Broadcasters rarely faced enforcement for failing to address issues of public importance in the first place. As a result, broadcasters could avoid the expense of defending enforcement actions by simply refusing to cover issues of public importance. As evidence, the Commission noted instances cited in the comments of planned coverage of issues of public importance being jettisoned for fear of Fairness Doctrine lawsuits,[31] as well as refusals on the part of broadcasters to carry certain paid programming that they feared would trigger their Fairness Doctrine obligations.[32]

The Commission could not determine, however, whether the Fairness Doctrine had been codified by Congress in Section 315 of the Communications Act.[33] The agency observed that the legislative language was ambiguous as to whether Congress had intended to approve the Commission's authority to enforce the doctrine or to create a new statutory requirement.[34] Evidence culled from the legislative history also was of little help in determining the intent of Section 315.[35] Furthermore, pending before Congress at the time were bills related to the Fairness Doctrine. Accordingly, the FCC declined to repeal the doctrine in 1985, and chose to wait for further guidance from Congress on the issue.[36] Despite declining to repeal the doctrine, the agency made clear its belief that the most effective way to encourage the free exchange of ideas over broadcast was to have an open and unregulated marketplace of ideas.

In 1986, the U.S. Court of Appeals for the District of Columbia held that Congress had not codified the Fairness Doctrine.[37] Section 315, according to the court, "ratified the Commission's longstanding position that the public interest standard authorize[d] the Fairness Doctrine," but did not "create [or] impose any obligation" on the Commission to enforce the Fairness Doctrine.[38] The Supreme Court declined to review this case.

Following this decision, Congress directed the FCC to examine alternatives to the Fairness Doctrine and to submit a report to Congress on the subject.[39] The FCC opened a proceeding seeking public comment on alternative means of administration and enforcement of the Fairness Doctrine.[40] Alternatives were analyzed including abandoning a case-by-case enforcement approach, replacing the doctrine with open access time for all members of the public, doing away with the personal attack rule, and eliminating certain other aspects of the doctrine.[41] The Commission rejected each of these alternatives for various reasons. This, however, was not the proceeding in which the Commission repealed the Fairness Doctrine.

The repeal of the doctrine occurred later in 1987. In a complaint against the television station WTVH Syracuse, NY, the FCC declined to sanction the broadcast station for a violation of the Fairness Doctrine, because the agency determined that the Fairness Doctrine violated the First Amendment.[42] The FCC repeated its findings from its 1985 report and argued that the scarcity rationale underpinning the Supreme Court's *Red Lion* decision was no longer valid. The agency also noted that

> the doctrine's affirmative use of government power to expand broadcast debate would seem to raise a striking paradox, for freedom of speech has traditionally implied an absence of governmental supervision or control. Throughout most of our history, the principal function of the First Amendment has been to protect the free marketplace of ideas by precluding government intrusion.[43]

The Fairness Doctrine, on the other hand, requires the government to make subjective judgments regarding which issues are of public importance and which points of view on those issues are significant enough to require broadcasters to cover them. The Commission expressed discomfort with its role in the editorial decisions being made by broadcasters and posited that such government involvement in these decisions ran contrary to the First Amendment.[44]

The Commission noted that many of the regulations it applies to broadcasters would be unconstitutional if applied to print media. The Commission also recognized, however, that speech restrictions placed upon broadcasters were subject to a lesser degree of constitutional scrutiny than restrictions placed on print media. The agency therefore conducted its analysis of the constitutionality of the Fairness Doctrine under the standard set forth in *Red Lion* and examined whether the Fairness Doctrine was "narrowly tailored to achieve a substantial government interest."[45]

The Fairness Doctrine was promulgated and enforced by the Commission in order to serve the public interest in access to an open and robust marketplace of ideas. The Commission had determined that the doctrine chilled the speech of broadcasters and inhibited free and open debate on the public airwaves. In the Commission's estimation, therefore, the Fairness Doctrine actually disserved the public interest and did not advance the substantial government interest in ensuring public access to diverse debate on the airwaves.[46] The Commission further argued that the Supreme Court should reconsider its application of a lower degree of First Amendment protection to broadcasters and that the First Amendment should protect media equally regardless of their delivery method.[47] This case was appealed to the D.C. Circuit Court of Appeals. The court upheld the order of the FCC, but did not reach the constitutional issue.[48]

CONSTITUTIONAL ISSUES

Application of the Fairness Doctrine to Broadcast Licensees

Because of the FCC ruling determining that the Fairness Doctrine violated the First Amendment, it is likely that any reinstatement of the doctrine, either by Congress or by the FCC, would be met by a court challenge on First Amendment grounds. Such a challenge may reach the Supreme Court of the United States, inviting the Court to reconsider *Red Lion*. In reviewing the constitutionality of the Fairness Doctrine as applied to broadcast licensees, the Court would likely be faced with two questions: (1) what standard of constitutional scrutiny to apply, and (2) whether the Fairness Doctrine withstands the chosen level of scrutiny.

Standard of Scrutiny

Government restrictions upon speech that are dependent upon the content of that speech are normally accorded strict scrutiny, the highest level of constitutional analysis and the most difficult for a law to survive.[49] The Fairness Doctrine is a content-based restriction on speech because it requires a government agent, the FCC, to examine the speech of private actors and to make subjective judgments regarding the fairness of the speech. In most circumstances, such a restriction would be reviewed under strict scrutiny, which requires the government to prove that the law is necessary to achieve a compelling government interest, and that the law is the least restrictive means of achieving that interest.[50] The Supreme Court has struck down laws similar to the Fairness Doctrine when applying strict scrutiny.[51] It seems, therefore, that if the Supreme Court were to apply strict scrutiny to the Fairness Doctrine the doctrine would be struck down.

In *Red Lion*, however, the Supreme Court determined that restrictions on the speech of broadcasters should be accorded a lesser standard of constitutional scrutiny, known as intermediate scrutiny.[52] Intermediate scrutiny requires the government to prove that the restriction on speech advances a substantial government interest and that the law is narrowly tailored (though not necessarily the least restrictive alternative) to achieve that interest. The Supreme Court reasoned that the scarcity of broadcast spectrum and the need to assure public access to a variety of viewpoints over the broadcast spectrum provided a basis for applying intermediate scrutiny in these circumstances.[53]

The FCC argued in its 1987 decision that the scarcity rationale was no longer applicable.[54] The agency noted an increase in the number of broadcast stations since the *Red Lion* decision. The agency also noted the increase in information sources and viewpoints available to the public via cable and satellite channels. Today, a party arguing against the scarcity rationale could take note of the dramatic increase in the ease of the communication of ideas via the Internet. It could be argued that these technological advances render the scarcity rationale obsolete.

The Supreme Court has had the opportunity to address this argument repeatedly and has consistently reaffirmed the validity of the scarcity rationale.[55] Despite the increased number of broadcast outlets and the increase in methods of mass information delivery (including cable, satellite, and the Internet), the fact remains, according to the Court, that not every individual who wishes to operate a broadcast station may do so.[56] The Supreme Court also has said that broadcast content is unique in American media.[57] It is free over the air to anyone with a television or a radio within range of a signal.

Broadcast, therefore, is distinct from cable, satellite, and the Internet, which are all services for which consumers must pay. Another possible reason the court may be disinclined to repudiate the scarcity rationale is the increased consolidation in ownership of media outlets, including broadcast stations.[58] If many of the broadcast stations across the country are owned by the same few large corporations, the argument that there exists an increased number of information sources in the broadcast marketplace may be more difficult for the Court to accept.

It is possible that, in light of the proliferation of different types of media outlets since *Red Lion*, the Supreme Court will abandon the scarcity rationale for applying a lower standard of scrutiny to restrictions on broadcasters' speech. If the scarcity rationale is abandoned, the Court will likely begin to apply strict scrutiny to broadcaster speech restrictions like the Fairness Doctrine. Because the Supreme Court has struck down regulations similar to the Fairness Doctrine when applied to other types of media, it seems unlikely that the Fairness Doctrine would survive review under strict scrutiny.[59]

It is also possible that the Supreme Court will maintain the scarcity rationale for applying a lower standard of scrutiny to restrictions on broadcasters' speech and will continue to apply intermediate scrutiny to the Fairness Doctrine.

The Constitutionality of the Fairness Doctrine as Applied to Broadcast Licensees

Assuming that the Supreme Court would continue to apply intermediate scrutiny to government restrictions on broadcasters' speech, the Court would then need to decide whether the Fairness Doctrine withstands such scrutiny. The Court may choose to uphold *Red Lion* and the Fairness Doctrine under the principle of *stare decisis*, which requires courts to adhere to precedent.[60] The Court also may choose to analyze a newly established Fairness Doctrine in light of evidence regarding its effects on speech that has developed since the *Red Lion* decision. To do so, it would have to answer two questions: (1) whether the Fairness Doctrine advances a substantial government interest, and (2) whether the doctrine is narrowly tailored to achieve that interest.

Substantial Interest

The government has a well-established substantial interest in ensuring access of the public to a diversity of viewpoints and information sources in a robust marketplace of ideas.[61] If the Supreme Court determines that the

Fairness Doctrine chills speech rather than encourages a robust exchange of ideas, it is likely that the Court would conclude that the Fairness Doctrine does not advance the government's interest in a well-informed citizenry and is unconstitutional. If, however, the Court finds that the Fairness Doctrine continues to advance a substantial government interest, the Court would move on to the next step in the constitutional analysis.

The Fairness Doctrine was originally promulgated under the FCC's authority to grant licenses to broadcasters that serve the public interest.[62] The public interest standard in the Communications Act necessarily implicates the First Amendment.[63] The Fairness Doctrine was intended to advance the government interest in ensuring the presence of a diversity of viewpoints over broadcast stations and to prevent broadcasters from monopolizing the airwaves with their personal interests.[64] Under this theory, the public's right to receive information would be protected from any tendency on the part of broadcasters only to communicate information of which they approved or agreed. Citing this reasoning, the Supreme Court, in *Red Lion*, upheld the constitutionality of the Fairness Doctrine.

Opponents of the Fairness Doctrine have argued that the doctrine actually inhibits the free exchange of ideas over the broadcast airwaves. The *Red Lion* Court noted in particular that, at the time the decision was rendered, there was no evidence that the Fairness Doctrine chilled speech.[65] The Court observed that, if such a theory were proven true, the FCC was not powerless to insist that broadcasters give coverage to issues of public importance.

In its 1985 report and 1987 decision repealing the doctrine, the FCC cited numerous instances in which broadcasters claimed to have refused to air certain pieces or cover issues for fear of Fairness Doctrine enforcement.[66] The agency further noted that the cost of defending Fairness Doctrine complaints could amount to significant sums of money and manpower, and could deter coverage of issues of public importance even further.[67] The FCC also noted the disparity between enforcement of the first prong of the doctrine (which requires coverage of issues of public importance) and the second prong (which requires significant views on those issues to be given fair coverage).[68] The agency explained that its own difficulty in enforcing the first prong arose because it received far fewer complaints regarding the failure to cover an important issue. Therefore, broadcasters could avoid enforcement actions for violations of the Fairness Doctrine by simply not covering the issue of public importance at all. The FCC may not be able to rectify this enforcement disparity in a cost-efficient manner, because any solution would require the agency to monitor the programming of all broadcasters at all times and to know which issues are of most importance to which communities. Such constant and far-reaching oversight may be beyond the capacity of any agency.

However, unlike other regulations on broadcaster speech that have been struck down, the Fairness Doctrine requires that speech be answered with more speech.[69] This aspect of the doctrine has been cited approvingly by the Supreme Court. The Fairness Doctrine does not single out any one point of view as objectionable or off-limits.[70] Instead, it requires that all significant points of view on issues of public importance receive broadcast time. This is a tenet at the core of the First Amendment, and it could be argued that the doctrine achieved its goal of raising the level of debate on the broadcast airwaves, despite the FCC's findings in the 1980s.

If the Supreme Court is persuaded by the argument that the Fairness Doctrine chills speech rather than encourages a robust exchange of ideas, the Court may find that the doctrine does not advance the government's interest in a well-informed citizenry. If the Court finds the doctrine does not advance that substantial government interest, the Court will strike it down as unconstitutional. If, however, the Court is persuaded by the argument it accepted in *Red Lion* (that the Fairness Doctrine advances the substantial government interest in a robust marketplace of ideas), the Court would move on to the next step in the constitutional analysis.

Narrow Tailoring

The next question the Court would address is whether the Fairness Doctrine would be narrowly tailored to achieve the government's interest. Under the previous enforcement regime the FCC examined each potential violation of the Fairness Doctrine on a case-by-case basis.[71] This tactic led to a measure of flexibility in penalties for violators and in the evolution of the doctrine.[72] Such flexibility enabled the Commission to be more responsive in its enforcement and to tailor each enforcement proceeding to the facts at issue in each case. In upholding the previous regime, the Supreme Court noted that it did not approve of each and every application of the Fairness Doctrine, but, because of the chosen method of enforcement, such approval was not required to uphold the doctrine in general.[73] If this enforcement regime is chosen once again, it is likely that the Court will follow its reasoning in *Red Lion* and deem the doctrine to be narrowly tailored. However, other methods of enforcement that are less well tailored are conceivable, and have been considered by the FCC.[74] Whether the Fairness Doctrine as newly established would be narrowly tailored will therefore depend upon the enforcement regime chosen by Congress or the FCC.

Application of the Fairness Doctrine to Cable and Satellite Providers

It does not appear that the Fairness Doctrine may be applied constitutionally to cable or satellite service providers. The Supreme Court has held that content-based restrictions on the speech of cable and satellite providers are subject to strict scrutiny.[75] Strict scrutiny requires that the restriction at issue advance a compelling government interest and that the restriction be the least restrictive means of achieving that interest.

Content-based regulations of speech in the print media are accorded strict scrutiny. The Supreme Court has recognized that regulations similar to the Fairness Doctrine, when applied to the print media, are not constitutional.[76] If regulations similar to the Fairness Doctrine could not withstand strict scrutiny when applied to the print media, it appears unlikely that similar regulations would withstand such scrutiny when applied to cable or satellite providers.

Continuing Congressional Debate

Since the repeal of the Fairness Doctrine, debate among legislators regarding whether to reinstate the doctrine has continued. Below are the bills related to the Fairness Doctrine that were introduced in the most recent Congresses, as well as a discussion of the recent correspondence between the chairman of the House Subcommittee on Communications and Technology and Chairman Genachowski.

111th Congress

H.R. 226, Broadcaster Freedom Act of 2009

This bill would deprive the FCC of the authority to re-promulgate or reinstate the Fairness Doctrine.

S. 34, S. 62 Broadcaster Freedom Act of 2009

These bills are identical to the House bill of the same name.

S. 160, District of Columbia Voting Rights Act of 2009 (Engrossed as Agreed to or Passed by the Senate)

Section 10 of the District of Columbia Voting Rights Act of 2009, as it was passed by the Senate, would create a new section in the Communications Act, Section 303A. Section 303A would prevent the FCC from reinstituting "the requirement that broadcasters present or ascertain opposing viewpoints on issues of public importance" or "any similar requirement that broadcasters meet programming quotas or guidelines for issues of public importance."

Section 9 of the same bill makes clear that "[n]othing in section 303A shall be construed to limit the authority of the Commission regarding matters unrelated to a requirement that broadcasters present or ascertain opposing viewpoints on issues of public importance."

These sections, taken together, appear to prevent the FCC from reinstating the Fairness Doctrine, or any similar requirement upon broadcasters in the future.

112th Congress

H.R. 642, Broadcaster Freedom Act of 2011

This bill would deprive the FCC of the authority to re-promulgate or reinstate the Fairness Doctrine.

Commission Letter Regarding Repeal of Regulations

On May 31, 2011, Chairman Upton of the House Subcommittee on Communications and Technology, along with other members of the Energy and Commerce Committee, sent a letter to the chairman of the FCC urging the Commission to remove the rules in the Code of Federal Regulations that reference the Fairness Doctrine, as well as the political-editorial and personal attack rules (47 C.F.R. §§ 73.1910, 76.209, 76.1612, 76.1613).[77] While these rules are largely regarded as dead letters, the chairman, nonetheless, asked that, in light of President Obama's executive order asking agencies to remove unwarranted regulations, the Commission begin with removing these regulations that most agree should no longer be enforced.

On June 6, 2011, Chairman Julius Genachowski responded indicating that Commission staff is expected to recommend the removal of these regulations from the Code of Federal Regulations.[78] Chairman Genachowski also expressed his support for the removal of those regulations. The letter also identified a number of statutory provision that Congress might consider amending or removing due to their obsolescence.

End Notes

[1] *See* The Radio Act of 1927, P.L. 69-632, ch. 169, 44 Stat. 1162 (1927).
[2] 47 U.S.C. § 301.
[3] 47 U.S.C. § 307.
[4] 47 U.S.C. §§ 307, 309.
[5] 47 U.S.C. § 303.
[6] National Broadcasting Co. v. U.S., 319 U.S. 190, 219 (1943).
[7] 13 FCC Rept. 1246 (1949) [hereinafter "Report on Editorializing"].
[8] *Id.*
[9] Applicability of the Fairness Doctrine in the Handling of Controversial Issues of Public Importance, 29 Fed. Reg. 10426 (1964).
[10] Report on Editorializing, 13 FCC at 1249.
[11] *Id.*
[12] This obligation is widely referred to as the Cullman Doctrine, because it originated in the FCC decision *Cullman Broadcasting Co.*, 40 FCC 576 (1976).
[13] 47 C.F.R. §§ 73.123, 73.300, 73.598, 73.679.
[14] *Id.*
[15] 47 U.S.C. § 315; 47 C.F.R. § 73.1910 (1985).
[16] H.Rept. 86-1069, 86th Cong., 1st sess., August 27, 1959 at 5.
[17] Applicability of the Fairness Doctrine in the Handling of Controversial Issues of Public Importance, 29 Fed. Reg. 10416 (1964).
[18] *Id.*
[19] *See* In the Matter of Inquiry into Section 73.1910 of the Commission's Rules and Regulations Concerning Alternatives to the General Fairness Doctrine Obligations of Broadcast Licensees, 2 FCC Rcd 5272 (1987).
[20] 395 U.S. 367 (1969).
[21] *Id.* at 371-373.
[22] *Id.* at 375-386.
[23] Great Lakes Broadcasting Co., 3 F.R.C. Ann. Rep. 32, 33 (1929), *rev'd on other grounds*, 37 F.2d 993, cert. dismissed, 281 U.S. 706 (1930).
[24] Report on Editorializing, 13 FCC at 1246 - 1270.
[25] *Id.* at 390 (citations omitted).
[26] General Fairness Doctrine Obligations of Broadcast Licensees, Report, 50 Fed. Reg. 35418 (1985).
[27] *Id.*
[28] *Id.* at 35420.
[29] *Id.*
[30] *Id.* at 35422.

[31] For example, the Commission cited a Southern California radio station that decided not to air a series on religious cults despite having already invested resources in its preparation. The decision, according to the radio station, was based upon the assessment of costs related to a potential Fairness Doctrine challenge. *Id.* at 35427.

[32] Specifically, the Commission cited comments from organizations such at the Glass Packaging Institute and the National Rifle Association. These commenters had documented difficulty in placing advertisements related to ballot measures due to Fairness Doctrine concerns. *Id.* at 35429.

[33] *Id.* at 35453.

[34] *Id.* at 35448.

[35] *Id.* at 35449. The Senate Committee Report provided that

> In recommending this legislation, the committee does not diminish or affect in any way Federal Communications Commission policy or existing law which holds that a licensee's statutory obligation to serve the public interest is to include the broad-encompassing duty of providing a fair cross-section of opinion ... S.Rep.No. 562, 86th Cong., 1st Sess. at 13 (1959).

This language appears to suggest that Congress did not intend to codify the Fairness Doctrine. However, in debate on the floor, some Members indicated their belief that the Fairness Doctrine amendment would codify the doctrine. One Member said, for example, that the Fairness Doctrine amendment "was the one condition we could write into the law to make sure the Federal Communications Commission would give the matter the right interpretation." 105 Cong. Rec. 17,778 (1959).

[36] 50 Fed. Reg. at 35453.

[37] Telecommunications Research and Action Center v. Federal Communications Commission, 801 F.2d 501, 516 (1986); cert. denied, 482 U.S. 919 (1987).

[38] Id. 517-518.

[39] Making Continuing Appropriations for Fiscal Year 1987, P.L. 99-500. *See also*, Conference Report to Accompany H.J.Res. 738, H.Rept. 99-1005. 99th Cong., 2d Sess. (1986).

[40] Inquiry into Section 73.1910 of the Commission's Rules and Regulations Concerning Alternatives to the General Fairness Doctrine Obligations of Broadcast Licensees in MM Docket No. 97-26, 2 FCC Rcd 1532 (1987).

[41] In the Matter of Inquiry into Section 73.1910 of the Commission's Rules and Regulations Concerning Alternatives to the General Fairness Doctrine Obligations of Broadcast Licensees. 2 FCC Rcd 5272 (1987).

[42] In re Complaint of Syracuse Peach Council against Television Station WTVH Syracuse, New York, 2 FCC Rcd 5043 (1987).

[43] *Id.* at 5056.

[44] *Id.* at 5044.

[45] *Id.* at 5049.

[46] *Id.*

[47] *Id.* at 5058.

[48] Syracuse Peace Council v. FCC, 867 F.2d 654 (D.C. Cir. 1988).

[49] Sable Communications of California, Inc. v. Federal Communications Commission, 492 U.S. 115, 126 (1986).

[50] *Id.*

[51] *See* Miami Herald Publishing Co. v. Tornillo, 418 U.S. 241 (1974) (invalidating a Florida law that required newspapers to allow individuals space to reply to attacks made against them in the publication).

[52] *Red Lion*, 395 U.S. at 386.

[53] *Id.*; Columbia Broadcasting System Inc. v. Democratic National Committee, 412 U.S. 94, 101 (1973) (holding that [broadcast] frequencies are a scarce resource).

[54] *In re Complaint of Syracuse Peace Council*, 2 FCC Rcd at 5048.

[55] *See e.g.* FCC v. League of Women Voters, 468 U.S. 364 (1984) (striking down a ban on editorializing by noncommercial broadcasters); FCC v. Pacifica Foundation, 438 U.S. 726 (1978) (upholding regulations of indecent content over broadcast).

[56] *CBS v. FCC*, 412 U.S. at 101.

[57] *FCC v. Pacifica Foundation*, 438 U.S. at 748-749 (noting that broadcast stations have established a uniquely pervasive presence in the lives of all Americans).

[58] *See*, Free Press, Who Owns the Media? http://www.freepress.net/resources/ownership.

[59] *See FCC v. Pacifica*, 438 U.S. at 748 (noting that the First amendment protects publishers from being required to print replies, but provides broadcasters with no such protections); *Miami v. Tornillo*, 418 U.S. at 241 (invalidating a law that required newspapers to allow individuals to respond to personal attacks).

[60] Black's Law Dictionary 661 (2d Pocket ed. 2001).

[61] Associated Press v. United States, 326 U.S. 1, 20 (1945); New York Times Co. v. Sullivan, 376 U.S. 254, 270 (1964); Abrams v. United States, 250 U.S. 616, 630 (1919) (Holmes, J., dissenting).

[62] In the Matter of Editorializing by Broadcast Licensees, 13 FCC 1246 (1949).

[63] FCC v. League of Women Voters, 468 U.S. at 377.

[64] *See* Report on Editorializing, 13 FCC at 1246.

[65] *Red Lion*, 395 U.S. at 393-394.

[66] *General Fairness Doctrine Obligations of Broadcast Licensees*, Report, 50 Fed. Reg. at 35418; *In re Complaint of Syracuse Peach Council against Television Station WTVH Syracuse, New York*, 2 FCC Rcd. at 5043.

[67] *General Fairness Doctrine Obligations of Broadcast Licensees*, Report, 50 Fed. Reg. at 35418.

[68] *Id.* at 35422.

[69] *See* FCC v. League of Women Voters, 468 U.S. at 372.

[70] *See Applicability of the Fairness Doctrine in the Handling of Controversial Issues of Public Importance*, 29 Fed. Reg. at 10416.

[71] In the Matter of Inquiry into Section 73.1910 of the Commission's Rules and Regulations Concerning Alternatives to the General Fairness Doctrine Obligations of Broadcast Licensees, 2 FCC Rcd 5272 (1987).

[72] *Applicability of the Fairness Doctrine in the Handling of Controversial Issues of Public Importance*, 29 Fed. Reg. at 10416.

[73] *Red Lion*, 395 U.S. at 396.

[74] *See In the Matter of Inquiry into Section 73.1910 of the Commission's Rules and Regulations Concerning Alternatives to the General Fairness Doctrine Obligations of Broadcast Licensees*, 2 FCC Rcd at 5272.

[75] United States v. Playboy Entertainment Group, Inc., 529 U.S. 803, 813 (2000).

[76] *See FCC v. Pacifica*, 438 U.S. at 748 (noting that the First amendment protects publishers from being required to print replies, but provides broadcasters with no such protections); Miami v. Tornillo, 418 U.S. at 241 (invalidating a law that required newspapers to allow individuals to respond to personal attacks).

[77] Letter from Rep. Fred Upton, Chairman, House Subcommittee on Communications and Technology, to the Honorable Julius Genachowski, Chairman, Federal Communications Commission (May 31, 2011) *available at* http://republicans.energycommerce.house. Gov /Media/file/Letters/112th/053111fccfairnessdoctrine.pdf.

[78] Letter from the Honorable Julius Genachowski, Chairman, Federal Communications Commission to Rep. Fred Upton, Chairman, House Subcommittee on Communications and Technology (June 6, 2011) *available at* http://republicans.energycommerce.house.gov/ Media/file/Letters/112th/060611fccfairnessdoctrine.pdf.

INDEX

Q

R

S